LAW, CRIME AND LAW ENFORCEMENT

# POLICING

# STRATEGIES, MANAGEMENT AND POTENTIAL RISKS

# LAW, CRIME AND LAW ENFORCEMENT

Additional books in this series can be found on Nova's website
under the Series tab.

Additional e-books in this series can be found on Nova's website
under the eBooks tab.

LAW, CRIME AND LAW ENFORCEMENT

# POLICING

# STRATEGIES, MANAGEMENT AND POTENTIAL RISKS

JESSIE INGRAM
EDITOR

nova publishers
*New York*

## NOTICE TO THE READER



**Library of Congress Cataloging-in-Publication Data**

ISBN: 978-1-63485-369-9

*Published by Nova Science Publishers, Inc. † New York*

# CONTENTS

# PREFACE

This book discusses strategies, management and potential risks of policing. Chapter One describes and examines the 'Policing Excellence' and 'Prevention First' programs, and will discuss their successes and challenges since their introduction in 2009 in New Zealand. Chapter Two analyzes the action of the Military Police of Minas Gerais (PMMG) during the World Cup protests carried out in 2013 and 2014 in the state capital Belo Horizonte, Brazil. Chapter Three examines the emerging problem of cyber terrorism. It x-rays the concept of cyber terrorism as well as the tenor of existing scholarship on how to police it; and discusses the scope and ramifications of the problem and proposes a model for effectively policing Africa's terror-genic cyberspace.

Chapter 1 – Since the 1980s, the New Zealand Police have attempted to introduce a number of change management programs to improve the efficiency and the effectiveness of their core services, including: 'Project Blueprint,' 'Policing 2000,' 'Policing Excellence' and 'Prevention First.' The latest change management programs, 'Policing Excellence' and 'Prevention First' arose from three circumstances that were placing pressure on the delivery of policing services: (1) the impact of the 2007 global financial crisis on public sector funding and budgets; (2) the unsustainable increases in the demand for police services; and (3) the need for the police to modernize and lift productivity through the better use of technology. The New Zealand Police's operating environment had become increasingly complex in the decade prior to the 2007 global crisis. The crime rate, however, had been declining, but the actual social cost of crime was increasing. The New Zealand Government viewed the situation as unsustainable as the escalating costs were placing a heavy burden on the wider justice sector, with those costs increasing 79 percent between 1999 and 2009. At the same time, the demand for police services had increased, which reflected the changes in the social, demographic and economic conditions. In response to these pressures, the New Zealand Police identified a number of opportunities that could potentially increase productivity and deliver efficient, sustainable services. These opportunities were developed and implemented under two separate programs: 'Policing Excellence' and 'Prevention First.' This chapter will describe and examine these programs, and will discuss their successes and challenges since their introduction in 2009.

Chapter 2 – In this paper, the authors analyze the action of the Military Police of Minas Gerais (PMMG) during World Cup protests carried out in 2013 and 2014 in state capital Belo Horizonte. From direct observation of the policing standard adopted in those events, as well as interviews with those responsible for public safety policy, this paper problematizes the excessive use of force, characteristic of military operations, displayed in those moments. The pattern of operation developed by the Military Police during the protests is more characteristic of a war, highlighting the weight of the military uniform as a determinant of police behavior in Belo Horizonte.

Chapter 3 – Terrorists' use of internet infrastructure for the advancement of their agendas is an emerging problem that has elicited serious global concern. Critical national infrastructure such as electricity generation, telecommunications, transportation systems, financial services, gas/oil production, emergency and security services are increasingly depending on computer networks and are now vulnerable to attack by terrorist organizations. However, most researches on terrorism have tended to focus on traditional classical, real world terrorism, while cyber terrorism is relegated to the background culminating in a dearth of research in the area. This chapter attempts to bridge that gap by critically examining the emerging problem of cyber terrorism. The chapter x-rays the concept of cyber terrorism as well as the tenor of existing scholarship on how to police it. It discusses the scope and ramifications of the problem and proposes a model for effectively policing Africa's terror-genic cyberspace. The proposed policing strategy may work for countries faced with the growing threat of cyber terrorism who share similar demographics with developing countries of Africa.

In: Policing
Editor: Jessie Ingram

ISBN: 978-1-63485-369-9


*Chapter 1*

# ARE THE STRATEGIES OF "POLICING EXCELLENCE" AND "PREVENTION FIRST" NEW APPROACHES TO POLICE SERVICE DELIVERY IN NEW ZEALAND?

***Garth den Heyer****
Lecturer, Walden University and Senior Research Fellow, Police Foundation, Washington DC, US

## ABSTRACT

Since the 1980s, the New Zealand Police have attempted to introduce a number of change management programs to improve the efficiency and the effectiveness of their core services, including: 'Project Blueprint,' 'Policing 2000,' 'Policing Excellence' and 'Prevention First.' The latest change management programs, 'Policing Excellence' and 'Prevention First' arose from three circumstances that were placing pressure on the delivery of policing services: (1) the impact of the 2007 global financial crisis on public sector funding and budgets; (2) the unsustainable increases in the demand for police services; and (3) the need for the police to modernize and lift productivity through the better use of technology. The New Zealand Police's operating environment had

* gdenheyer@policefoundation.org.

become increasingly complex in the decade prior to the 2007 global crisis. The crime rate, however, had been declining, but the actual social cost of crime was increasing. The New Zealand Government viewed the situation as unsustainable as the escalating costs were placing a heavy burden on the wider justice sector, with those costs increasing 79 percent between 1999 and 2009. At the same time, the demand for police services had increased, which reflected the changes in the social, demographic and economic conditions. In response to these pressures, the New Zealand Police identified a number of opportunities that could potentially increase productivity and deliver efficient, sustainable services. These opportunities were developed and implemented under two separate programs: 'Policing Excellence' and 'Prevention First.' This chapter will describe and examine these programs, and will discuss their successes and challenges since their introduction in 2009.

## INTRODUCTION

In mid-2009, the New Zealand Police held a number of workshops to examine how the organization could respond to the changed fiscal and operating environment, and how it could improve the efficiency and the effectiveness of their service delivery. The 2007 global financial crisis had impacted the police budget and at the same time, there was an unsustainable increase in the demand for police services (New Zealand Police, 2014). Coupled with these issues was the need for the police to modernize and lift productivity through the better use of technology.

The New Zealand Police are a national police service with an establishment of approximately 9,000 officers and 2,500 civilian employees (New Zealand Police, 2015) that are responsible for the full range of law enforcement services and investigations from minor criminal offending and traffic enforcement, to major and organized crimes (den Heyer, 2012; 2015). Policing in New Zealand in the 2000s had become increasingly complex, with the police becoming more involved in issues around high-end policing and cybersecurity. The operating costs of the police had doubled between 1999 and 2008, and were forecast to increase by another 22 percent by 2013 if significant changes were not made to the organization and methods of service delivery (New Zealand Police, 2009). The financial constraints experienced by the police were within the context of a declining crime rate, but the actual social cost of crime had been increasing at an exponential rate (New Zealand Police, 2014). The New Zealand Government viewed the situation as being unsustainable, and one that was placing a heavy burden on the wider criminal justice sector, with justice sector costs increasing 79 percent between 1999 and 2009 (New Zealand Police, 2014). At the same time, there was an increase in the demand for police services, which reflected the changes in social, demographic and economic conditions (New Zealand 2014).

This created the motivation for change in New Zealand policing and the need for the police to increase productivity and focus on delivering efficient, sustainable services. A number of workshops were held to examine alternative methods to increase productivity and improve the delivery of services. The first program developed from the workshops, was called 'Fit for the Future.' This was later re-named a 'Comprehensive Approach to Policing Excellence' (CAPE).

CAPE was based principally on a prevention approach to responding to the occurrence of crime and in putting victims and the safety of the public at the center of policing, thereby enabling the future demand for services to be managed (New Zealand Police, 2014). In 2010, CAPE provided the catalyst for the police to develop a medium to long-term change program to respond to the financial and service delivery pressures it was facing, the implementation of which would fundamentally change the way that the police operated. The new program would enable the police to allocate resources to respond to both emergencies and calls from the public, and to prevent crime. The change program was called 'Policing Excellence' and was based primarily on how the police perceived the demand for their services.

The chapter begins by outlining the political and financial environment that led to the development of 'Policing Excellence' and eventually to the implementation of 'Prevention First.' The chapter then explains the New Zealand Police Deployment Model, the component work streams and the links between these strategies and 'Policing Excellence.' Finally, the chapter will examine the effect that Policing Excellence and Prevention First programs have had on the delivery of police services and on the level of crime in New Zealand.

## New Zealand Government Priorities

The New Zealand Government outlined its priorities for the public sector and the police in two documents. The first, the *Better Public Services Report* outlined a number of strategic areas that would guide government agencies, including the police, to improve the effectiveness of their organizations and their services to the public. The four identified areas to be improved were:

delivering better results; better services and value-for-money; leadership will be critical; and quantifying the gains (State Services Commission, the Treasury and the Department of Prime Minister and Cabinet, 2012). The second document was the *Budget Policy Statement 2012*.

The priority setting documents offered a framework to assist the justice sector agencies to achieve the specified priorities. An action plan called *Delivering Better Public Services: Reducing Crime and Re-Offending Result Action Plan* stipulated four targets that the police were to achieve by June 2017:

- Reduce the crime rate by 15 percent
- Reduce the youth crime rate by 5 percent
- Reduce the violent crime rate by 20 percent
- Reduce the re-offending rate by 25 percent (State Services Commission, et al., 2012).

To achieve the four goals determined by the government, the police developed a number of priorities that would be achieved through the implementation of 'Policing Excellence' and the *Prevention First Operating Strategy*. The link between the improvement areas specified by the government and the police service delivery priorities and programs through which the policing priorities were to be implemented are presented in Table 1.

## New Zealand Government Performance Excellence Framework

The New Zealand Government developed a Performance Excellence Framework to help government agencies integrate their approach to organizational performance management and to provide the information necessary that would assist decision-makers to improve their agency's delivery of service. The implementation of the framework resulted in:

- an improvement in the services delivered;
- an increase in organizational effectiveness and capabilities; and
- an enhancement in organizational and personal learning (Cotter, 2007).

**Table 1. Matching Government Priorities to Police Priorities**

| | Government priorities | Police priorities |
|---|---|---|
| 1 | Deliver better public services | |
| | Reducing crime<br>Reducing the rate of total crime<br>Preventing corruption, fraud, organised crime and money laundering | Understanding and responding to the drivers of crime<br>Organised crime and drugs<br>Methamphetamine action plan<br>Alcohol |
| | Reduced youth crime | Youth Strategy |
| | Supporting vulnerable children<br>Reduce violent crime<br>Reduce the number of assaults on children | Family violence<br>Child abuse |
| | Improving interaction with the government | Putting victims and witnesses at the centre of our response<br>Victim focus – implement the Victims of Crime Reform Bill<br>Service excellence |
| 2 | Building a more competitive and productive economy | |
| | Keeping the road network safe and flowing freely | Road policing |
| 3 | Responsibly managing the Government's finances | Continuous improvement<br>Policing Excellence<br>Leadership excellence, direction and delivery<br>People development |
| | Managing within current funding levels | Finance and resource management<br>Performance Improvement Framework (PIF)<br>Change Programme |
| 4 | Rebuilding Christchurch | Cross sector initiatives |
| | Creating a public safety hub in Christchurch with other agencies | |

Adapted from New Zealand Police (2012a).

It was the government's intention that agencies would demonstrate elements of performance excellence which would align with an increase in customer satisfaction, stakeholder satisfaction, productivity, quality of service and staff retention. Attaining an improvement in these factors would be underpinned by quality process management, organisational effectiveness and the minimization of all forms of waste.

The Performance Excellence Framework was adapted by the police, which in turn, was termed the 'Police Achievement Framework.' The Police

Achievement Framework was comprised of seven categories that encapsulated the core values and concepts of the Performance Excellence Framework:

Leadership and Governance:

1. Community and Citizen;
2. Strategic Planning;
3. Policing Processes;
4. Police People;
5. Results; and
6. Intelligence, Evidence and Knowledge (Cotter, 2007).

The criteria documented in the Police Achievement Framework would therefore be used to assess the police and its various functional units on its ability to focus on results, create value, and continuously improve (Cotter, 2007).

## The Beginning: 'Policing Excellence'

The 'Policing Excellence' program commenced in August 2010 and included a series of initiatives that would enable the police to shift resources from responding to the occurrence of crime into prevention-focused activities. As a result of the rearrangement, it was envisaged that the police would be better able to manage future demand for services and that the reallocation of resources would result in the reduction of victimization and offending, and ultimately enhance public safety (New Zealand Police, 2011b; 2013d; 2014). The program was also to have a positive flow-on effect on the courts and the wider justice sector (New Zealand Police, 2014).

The basic premise of the Policing Excellence program was to generate productivity gains by managing frontline officer time more effectively; and to purposefully reinvest the realized frontline staff time into generating improved performance in crime prevention and victim focused activity (New Zealand Police, 2014). These principles were to be achieved through a new policing model called Prevention First and put prevention[1] at the forefront of

[1] Although it was not explicitly defined in any of the available New Zealand Police documents relating to the development of Policing Excellence and Prevention First, the expression 'prevention' in the New Zealand Police context does not only include the prevention of crime related events but also other social ills that the police respond to. For example, the police have extensive input into the design of policies and legislation relating to such issues

everything that the police did. However, although prevention was the primary strategy of this new approach, it was to be balanced with the ability to respond to incidents of crime, undertake investigations and implement resolutions. The program was to be based on a nationally coordinated approach, and not only was it designed to reduce operating costs, but it was to be the main strategy for the police to achieve the three outcomes that the government expected the police to achieve by 2014/15:

- a 13 percent decrease in recorded crime;
- a 19 percent decrease in the number of prosecutions; and
- a 4 percent increase in the Police's prevention output (New Zealand Police, 2012b).

The Policing Excellence change program initially consisted of 11 work streams, each of which was led by a District Commander (New Zealand, 2014). The initial 11 work streams were:

1. Police Model
   a. Prevention First
   b. Deployment
   c. Victim Focus
   d. Performance Management
   e. Productivity (Continuous Improvement)
2. Case Management
3. Alternative Resolutions
4. Crime Reporting Line
5. Rostering to Reduce Demand
6. Cost Recovery
7. Mobility
8. Support Services to the Frontline
9. Policing Act Opportunities
10. Asset Management
11. Performance Management (New Zealand Police, 2013d; 2014).

The program comprised of four specific stages; initiation, design and build, implementation/execution, and embedding and benefit realization. The

as violence to women. In this way, the issue of prevention is not about preventing the offence from occurring but more about preventing the social environment that creates the situation for the offence to occur.

four stages of the program and the year of their implementation are presented in Table 2.

**Table 2. Policing Excellence Implementation Timeline**

| | Stage | Year | Explanation |
|---|---|---|---|
| 1 | Programme Initiation | 2009/10 | Each work stream separately developed an outline plan and Stage 1 business case relating to their specific Policing Excellence initiative. |
| 2 | Programme Design and Build | 2010/11 | Each work stream developed specifications for their initiative and, where necessary, a pilot and an evaluation completed. This resulted in the development of Stage 2 business cases and other supporting articles. |
| 3 | Programme Implementation/Execution | 2011/12/13 | Each work stream developed charters/implementation plans and the implementation of initiatives commenced. |
| 4 | Embedding and Benefit Realization | 2013/14/15 | Each work stream transitions to the business (embedding) and the benefits realised. |

Adapted from New Zealand Police (2014).

To assist with the transitioning from the design stage of the program to the implementation phase, in late 2011, the responsibility of leading the 11 work streams was transferred from the District Commanders to the national police headquarters, and the responsibility for leading the implementation of the work streams was assigned to the respective districts. To assist the districts with the implementation stage and to ensure that efficiencies would be realized, the police developed a comprehensive benefit-management approach, which was based on two benefit classes:

1. Productivity: involving officer and staff hours, full-time equivalents or finances released for more productive use; and

2. Performance: concentrating on reducing recorded crime through the focus on: the 'crime triangle' (victims, offenders, locations) and the five drivers of crime[2] (New Zealand Police, 2014).

## THE NEXT STAGE: THE 'PREVENTION FIRST' STRATEGY

In December 2011, the police launched the *Prevention First: The National Operating Strategy 2011 – 2015* (New Zealand Police, 2011b). The strategy is the central element of the Police Model and contained three pillars which provided operational linkages with a modified version of John Eck's crime triangle[3] (New Zealand Police, 2011b). The basic tenet of the strategy was crime prevention and putting the needs of victims at the front of New Zealand policing by "having the right people in the right place at the right time," thereby preventing crime before it could occur (New Zealand Police, 2014). Figure 1 presents the linkages between the crime triangle and the three pillars of the strategy:

1. Deployment to reduce public demand (entitled "beat demand");
2. Understanding and responding to the five drivers of crime; and
3. Developing a change in thinking to that which puts prevention and the needs of victims at the forefront of policing (New Zealand Police, 2011b).

The Prevention First program was designed to provide guidance to reduce the occurrence of crime and simultaneously improve the effectiveness of the delivery of police services. The improvement in service delivery performance was to be achieved by reinvesting saved time into crime prevention activities (New Zealand Police, 2011b). All staff were to seek out prevention opportunities as a part of their daily work and were encouraged to look beyond single issues associated with individual cases or events (New Zealand Police, 2011b).

---

[2] In 2013, the New Zealand Police identified the five drivers of crime in New Zealand as families, youth, Alcohol, road policing, and organized crime and drugs (New Zealand Police, 2013b).

[3] See Cullen, F., Eck, J., & Lowenkamp, C. (2002). Environmental corrections: A new paradigm for effective supervision. Federal Probation, 66(2), 28–37.

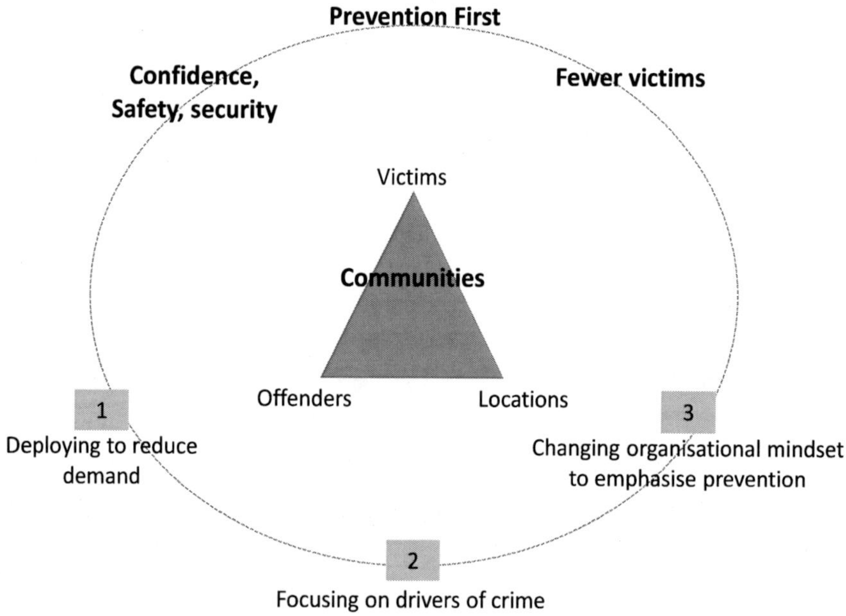


Figure 1. Linkage between the Crime Triangle and Prevention First's Three Strategic Pillars.

The principle method that the police adopted to ensure the success of the strategy was the development of stronger partnerships, especially with other government agencies and, more importantly, with members of the community. The development of stronger collaboration was to be achieved by working in partnership with the community, in particular, with Iwi[4] and other local service providers to address the over-representation of Maori[5] in the criminal justice system, as both victim and suspect (New Zealand Police, 2011b).

To operationalize the strategy, the police developed the National Tactical Plan (NTP) in 2012. The National Tactical Plan informed the police districts of the day-to-day operational protocols that supported the achievement of the Prevention First strategy, which assisted the police to meet the three outcomes specified by the government (New Zealand Police, 2011c).

---

[4] Iwi is a Maori community usually linked by family ties.

[5] Although Maori are only 14 percent of the New Zealand population, they account for more than 43 percent of criminal convictions, 47 percent of violent offending convictions and 51 percent of prison inmates (www.statistics.govt.nz).

The National Tactical Plan was designed to confront the five drivers of crime by identifying appropriate, local response tactics to minimize the occurrence of these crimes (New Zealand Police, 2011c).

The first National Tactical Plan 2013/14 came into effect on 1 January 2013 (New Zealand Police, 2014). It was designed to give 'back-to-basics' operational context and perspective to the Prevention First Operating Strategy by providing the districts with a number of tactical service delivery options (New Zealand Police, 2014). The plan outlined the five drivers of crime and placed an emphasis on the type of tactics to be deployed to address these drivers at the local level (New Zealand Police, 2014).

It was purported that many of the underlying issues of the five drivers of crime intersected and overlapped, and had an effect on each other. The police proposed that the drivers could be better addressed by taking a multi-agency and multi-disciplinary approach to identify possible solutions (New Zealand Police, 2014). This more collaborative approach to address the causes of the drivers of crime recognized that the National Tactical Plan would have more effect if the police cooperated with partner agencies. In addition to the collaborative approach, police staff needed to apply other strategic plans and initiatives when they were developing tactics, for example, those outlined in the National Road Policing Strategy (New Zealand Police, 2014).

While the National Tactical Plan prescribed operational tactics, it did not prescribe outputs or performance measures (New Zealand Police, 2011c). Rather, the National Tactical Plan guided the development of specific and focused police district tactical plans. It was the responsibility of the districts to determine how the tactics would be deployed and how the outcomes sought would be measured (New Zealand Police, 2011c). The districts were supported in their achievement of the desired goals by the implementation of a new performance management framework. However, it was acknowledged by national police headquarters that achieving the tactics contained within the district tactical plans would be more successful if a complete police approach was used while harnessing the additional support of partner agencies (New Zealand Police, 2011c). The planning structure for the National Tactical Plan and its relationship with the district planning structure is presented in Appendix A.

The second method used to implement the strategy was the establishment of four of the principal components of the Deployment Model. These primary components are:

- Tasking and Coordination – This is the key component of deployment and sits at the centre of the Deployment Model. The process is based on a modified Ratcliffe (2004) 3i intelligence model (influence, interpret and impact). The Ratcliffe 3i model describes the relationship between intelligence, decision-makers and the crime environment. This information informs the Tasking and Coordination process to ensure that deployment decisions are intelligence-led. The decision-making process is then used to set and agree national, district and area priorities, the assigning of tasks, the identification of accountabilities and the allocation of resources. The process is proactive and forward looking with an emphasis on longer-term outcomes and solutions.
- Critical Command Information – This is a substantial component of the Tasking and Coordination process and describes all of the information that decision-makers need to consider before deploying or allocating resources. The component includes five elements: intelligence, demand for services, actual strength, strategic priorities and performance management.
- Operational Delivery – This is the implementation of the tactics which were identified during the Tasking and Coordination process at the national, district and area level.
- Workforce Management – This delivers the resources to provide the capability and the capacity to be applied to achieve the tactics which were identified during the Tasking and Coordination process at the national, district and area levels (New Zealand Police, 2011c).

The four principle components of the Deployment Model are linked to the three pillars of the Prevention First strategy and provide the framework for focusing on specific prevention and proactive tactics and the methods to reduce offending and victimization.

## Tasking and Coordination

Tasking and Coordination is used at all three levels of the police (national, district and area) and is the process by which Critical Command Information is turned into prioritized, operational activity (New Zealand Police, n. d.). Tasking and Coordination is forward looking and proactive with an emphasis placed on outcomes and solutions (New Zealand Police, n. d.). The process is based on five principles:

1. The process follows a common operating philosophy, which promotes leadership, transparency and accountability.
2. The process uses Critical Command Information with the five drivers of crime to set priorities, make decisions, and own and coordinate deployment activities.
3. Participants adhere to the agreed meeting and tasking practices.
4. Participants embrace Prevention First through explicitly engaging with their community.
5. Participants recognise the delegated authority and accountability of areas and districts, and the authority of the Commissioner via the Deputy Commissioner: Operations to direct operational activity nationally (New Zealand Police, n. d.).

## The Deployment Model

The Deployment Model was pivotal to the implementation and the envisaged success of the Prevention First strategy. The model, presented in Figure 2, provided a structured framework, which enabled managers to efficiently and effectively deploy staff and resources to the local crime environment in a nationally-consistent manner (New Zealand Police, 2011d).

The model is founded on three principles: informed and directed taskings, a better understanding of demand and of police capabilities, and a clear focus on achieving the specified results. The model was developed to provide greater assurance in allocating and deploying resources (New Zealand Police, 2011d). The assurance was afforded through the process of predicting the demand in each district, matching this demand against the skills and availability of staff at any given time and using technology more effectively to "beat demand" (New Zealand Police, 2011d).

## District Command Centres

The District Command Centers are fundamental to the implementation of the Police Model and enable the police executive to have a more informed understanding of the operating environment in order to make real time resource allocation and deployment decisions. They are a vital operational component of the Deployment Model and ensure that police staff are deployed to the "right place at the right time to prevent crime and road trauma" (New Zealand Police, 2013a).

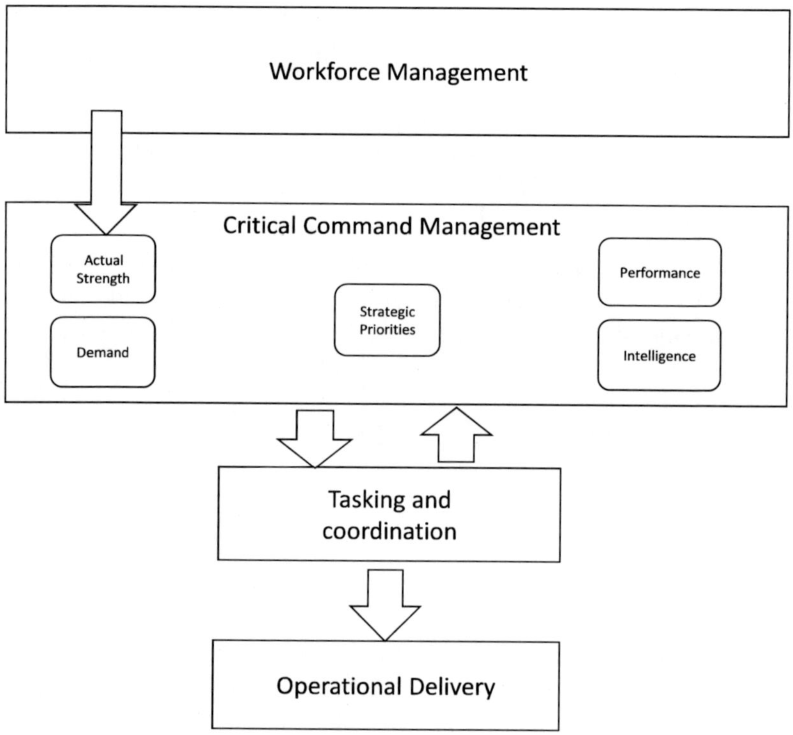


Adapted from New Zealand Police (2011d).

Figure 2. New Zealand Police Prevention First Deployment Model.

While the District Command Centers are responsible for effectively implementing the Deployment Model, they also assist with operationalizing other agency and Policing Excellence initiatives. They provide, for example, the platform for ongoing initiatives to meet the government's Better Public Service targets and the organization's strategic objectives, such as the Turning of the Tide Strategy[6]. These initiatives, together with the Prevention First Operating Strategy and the district tactical plans, drive the prevention-focused taskings from the District Command Centers. The use of the Critical

[6] This a strategy relating to working with Maori to minimize Maori offending.

Command Information picture is informed by the outputs of Policing Excellence initiatives, such as those provided from the Victim Focus Framework, Case Management and the Crime Reporting Line, as well as other police information sources, such as intelligence, demand profile, performance management and the human resource system (New Zealand Police, 2013a).

# OTHER WORK STREAMS THAT ENABLE PREVENTION FIRST

## Alternative Resolutions

The Alternative Resolutions work stream looked at the formalized use of discretion as an alternative to an individual being charged for an offence. It was envisaged that this would not only reduce the use of court processes for low-level offending, but also would ensure that the offending would still be addressed and give victims support. The implementation of this program gave officers the ability to use formalized warnings and to use greater discretion when dealing with an offender. This Policing Excellence work stream included the development and implementation of:

- Pre-Charge Warnings;
- Written Traffic Warnings; and
- Community Justice Panels.

It was these three options would serve to keep low-level, often first-time offenders, out of the justice system while ensuring that an action is taken in regard to the offending.

## Neighborhood Policing

Between 2010 and 2013, the police established 34 Neighborhood Policing Teams in prioritized locations throughout the country (New Zealand Police, 2013c). These teams focused primarily on reducing crime, preventing victimization, improving perceptions of safety, and increasing trust and confidence in the police. The teams were established so that they could work on problems and issues until the problems and issues are either eliminated or able to be handed back to the community for the community to manage themselves, without the need for further police intervention (New Zealand Police, 2013c). It was proposed that the Neighborhood Policing Teams would specifically target the underlying causes of crime and issues of safety wherever possible, through the leverage of community and partner agency resources (New Zealand Police, 2013c).

A Neighborhood Policing Team is usually comprised of between four and six constables and one sergeant and operates in their dedicated location for up to five years. The locations that the Neighborhood Policing Team operate from are determined by the use of a combination of statistical data, local knowledge and specifically developed intelligence products (New Zealand Police, 2013c). As well as their preventative role, Neighborhood Policing Teams also support frontline staff; respond to non-emergency calls for service; and work rosters that meet the needs of the neighborhood and address its specific problems (New Zealand Police, 2014).

## Family Violence Program

Minimizing family violence is one of the highest priorities of the New Zealand Police, and reducing the number of and the impact of family violence occurrences is a key component of the Prevention First Strategy (New Zealand Police, 2014). The intention of the program is to initiate changes in the organization which will improve the efficiency and the effectiveness of the police response, and the subsequent investigation into and the resolution of family violence (New Zealand Police, 2014).

The program consists of 10 specific projects to improve the response to family violence. It is envisaged that each of the project's objectives and deliverables will improve existing initiatives and will introduce new innovations for dealing with family violence. These 10 projects and their purpose are presented in Table 3.

## Victim Focus

The focus on victims is centre to the Prevention First Operating Strategy. The strategy is based on the proposal that by supporting victims, the likelihood of re-victimization can be significantly reduced, thereby reducing future demand on police's time and resources (New Zealand Police, 2014).

**Table 3. Family Violence Programme Projects**

| | Project | Details |
|---|---|---|
| 1 | Incident response | To develop improvements to the police initial response practices at a family violence incident. |
| 2 | Victims | To transform the services provided to family violence victims, with improved integration with the Victim Focus Framework (Graduated Response Model). |
| 3 | Offenders | To transform the services provided to family violence offenders, considering alternative actions, including restorative justice. |
| 4 | Risk assessment | To assess the current family violence risk assessment tools and to develop recommended options for their future use, to improve outcomes for victims and their families. |
| 5 | Family Safety Teams | To assess current Family Safety Team service delivery and recommend options for future deployment of Family Safety Team resources. |
| 6 | Data quality | To work with existing police systems to improve data capture and access to family violence data to assist in evidence based decision making at an area, district, and national level for quality responses to family violence. |
| 7 | Quality Assurance and Improvement Framework (QAIF) | To develop and implement a QAIF for family violence. This will assist with good management practice and early risk identification and ownership of issues in regards to family violence investigations and resolutions. |
| 8 | Mobility | To fully utilise mobility within the family violence environment to improve the quality and speed of police reporting, evidence collection, completion of risk assessments and referrals. This will allow frontline staff to focus on delivering quality services to the people involved, rather than completing paperwork at the scene. |
| 9 | Training | To develop effective training frameworks to foster a positive mindset, to ensure that all police employees complete an effective response or intervention to reduce family violence harm. |
| 10 | Our Practise | To improve support for police staff who may experience family violence in their lives. |

Adapted from New Zealand Police (2014).

A new victim-centric response model was piloted in two of the police districts before being implemented national-wide in December 2012 (New Zealand Police, 2014). The response model is based on a graduated three level response (bronze, silver or gold) that the victim may receive (New Zealand Police, 2014). The level of response provided by the police will depend on the specific requirements of the victim. The bronze response, for example, is the basic level of response that every victim would receive; whereas, a gold response is the highest level of response that a victim might receive and would be given to a victim with the greatest risk of repeat victimization (New Zealand Police, 2014). Fundamental to a gold response is the development and the implementation of a Victim Intervention Plan (New Zealand Police, 2014). A Victim Intervention Plan is specific to the needs of a victim and often involves the underlying causes of repeat victimization to be addressed by partner agencies (New Zealand Police, 2014).

## Case Management

Prior to the introduction of the Case Management work stream, there was no national file or case management strategy. Models for managing cases evolved in isolation and without alignment to any clearly defined file management practices and without any understanding of the future direction of file management (New Zealand Police, 2014).

Case Management was formally implemented as a part of the Policing Excellence program across all 12 districts between 2010 and 2013 and comprised of the development and the implementation of the Case Management Business Model. The model established a national business unit and four business units in each of the twelve districts:

- The Crime Reporting Line – A national facility, located in Auckland, which provides 24/7 reporting services to the whole country. The unit is responsible for the resolution of all crime that is reported through this channel in the first telephone call.
- File Management Centres – One unit per district, which is centrally based and provides support to the district. The centres receive and progress all new cases generated through the Crime Reporting Line, public counters, response staff and other sources. The responsibilities of the centre includes: quality control, case screening, victim feedback, referral for further investigation, and subsequent case closure administration.
- Investigation Support Units – One unit per district, which is centrally based and provides support to the district. Files are assigned by the district File Management Centre. The Investigation Support Unit conducts initial and follow-up enquiries for volume cases and other

cases as directed by the district. They undertake value-adding activities which include telephone enquiries, the examination of evidence and case assignment to inactivation/filing or referral to an area-based investigation unit.

- Criminal Justice Support Units – One or more units per district, which provides support to an area or a district. Units are responsible for the centralized preparation of prosecution files, including preparing witness and officer evidence statements, exhibit preparation, disclosure and case closure (Adapted from New Zealand Police, 2013e; 2014).

## Crime Reporting Line

The Crime Reporting Line is based on the concept of call-centers and it is aimed at providing the public with an accessible and efficient channel to police services for the reporting of historical and non-emergency crime (New Zealand Police, 2014). The establishment of the Crime Reporting Line allows for information to be accurately collected and recorded in a single point of contact (New Zealand Police, 2014).

Prior to the implementation of the Crime Reporting Line, the public primarily reported incidents of crime at local police stations or by telephone. This, along with other factors, such as increasing 111 call volumes, created an opportunity to improve telephone-based and web-based customer service (New Zealand Police, 2014).

## Police Approach to Collaboration

The long term objective of the national Prevention First: Operating Strategy is to sustainably reduce crime through partnerships and strategic opportunities (New Zealand Police, 2013b). The emphasis on developing strategic collaborations has enabled the police to focus their prevention efforts on the five drivers of crime: families, youth, alcohol, road policing and organized crime and drugs. Underlying these drivers are a range of social issues that necessitate the police to work in partnership with those agencies and institutions that have the skills and the ability to assist with the development of response plans (New Zealand Police, 2013b). This structure has been implemented because the police recognize that collaboration in the early intervention stages is most likely to produce the most effective outcomes (New Zealand Police, 2013b).

The establishment of a collaborative approach enables the police to employ community- based crime prevention approaches that encourage communities and other agencies to play key roles in addressing issues within their communities (New Zealand Police, 2013b). The targeted actions undertaken as a result of these efforts are intended to change the conditions in communities that are believed to sustain crime and to create a framework to encourage communities and other agencies to take ownership of the issues that exist in relation to the drivers of crime (New Zealand Police, 2013b).

## Performance Management Framework

Prior to the commencement of Policing Excellence in 2009, the performance framework of the police consisted of a five-year strategic plan, which was based on the direction of the government and an annual Statement of Intent. To enable the Policing Excellence work streams to be measured and to ensure that the police were receiving the benefits of these efforts, the police developed a performance management framework.

It was envisaged that the Performance Management Framework would provide an aggregated view of data from various sources to assist with operationalizing the Policing Excellence and the Prevention First: Operating Strategy (New Zealand Police, 2014). The framework would enable the districts to better forecast crime rates and to measure their operational performance by tracking their progress towards achieving their goals and targets – including the effectiveness of prevention-focused tactics and activities (New Zealand Police, 2014). It was also anticipated that the Performance Management Framework would provide the methodology for auditing the realization of benefits from the introduction of the Prevention First: Operating Strategy.

The current Performance Management Framework includes a number of inter-linking levels (political, national, district/group, unit, individual), goals, plans and priorities that offers an overview of the performance of the police across a range of activities (New Zealand Police, 2014). The range of activities incorporate the assessment of performance at input, output, impact and outcome levels, and identifies and analyzes a number of key indicators (New Zealand Police, 2014). The Performance Management Framework and its different levels are presented in Figure 3.

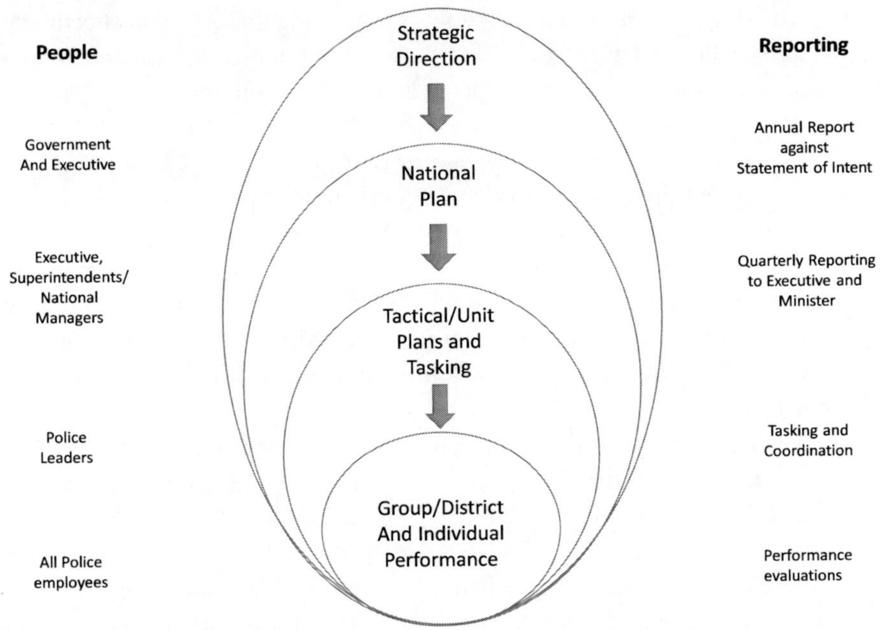


Adapted from New Zealand Police (2013f).

Figure 3. Planning and Performance from Government to Police Employee Framework – Known as 'the line of sight.'

## Continuous Improvement

The consideration and development of the Continuous Improvement work stream began in 2011. The police determined that Continuous Improvement was based on improvements in efficiency and productivity, and the work stream was implemented with the expectation that two sets of deliverables would be achieved:

1. *Under the Continuous Improvement Framework:*

- The development of a methodology which identifies the most efficient and value-added ways of providing continuous improvement and an improvement in service productivity at all levels of the policing business.

- The development of a methodology which identifies the most efficient and value-added ways of providing continuous improvement and service delivery improvements at all levels of policing.

2. *Under Centre for Continuous Improvement:*

- The development of a service of continuous improvement which will increase the level of productivity and service delivery and over time will allow for the greater investment in crime prevention. Existing systems, tools and processes will be utilized to capture and manage productivity improvement opportunities, which have been suggested by staff or that have resulted from issues affecting productivity or service levels.
- The development of a definition for the role, structure, and processes for the Centre for Continuous Improvement (New Zealand Police, 2014).

In late 2013, the police established a Centre for Continuous Improvement which was to implement a continuous improvement framework and develop an organizational culture that:

- actively engages frontline staff in identifying and implementing service delivery improvements; and
- optimizes the productivity, efficiency and effectiveness of policing services, including their user-friendliness and 'people focus' (New Zealand Police, 2014).

## CURRENT ARRANGEMENTS FOR ASSESSING THE PERFORMANCE OF THE POLICE

### A Performance Assessment Process for Policing Excellence

A governance framework was established to oversee, direct and monitor all of the embedding activities of the Policing Excellence work streams. Following the implementation of the Policing Excellence work streams, the police established a small team to manage and oversee the embedding of the work streams and to ensure that actual and anticipated benefits were delivered and reinvested as intended. The team developed an embedding plan and a framework based on the following five principles:

1. Embedding criteria: clear and unambiguous;
2. Command Assessment Round 1 and 2 (CA R1 and R2);
3. Active Governance;
4. Continuous Improvement; and
5. Communication (New Zealand Police, 2014).

As a part of the embedding plan, work stream owners developed specific embedding criteria for each work stream (New Zealand Police, 2014). The purpose of the embedding criteria was to set clear expectations for staff and the districts, identify measures and specify the end state for each of the work streams (New Zealand Police, 2014).

A colored dashboard system was introduced, which enabled the police executive to monitor the progress of the embedding plan. The dashboard not only provided the opportunity to monitor the progress of the embedding of the work streams it also assisted the executive to identify risk or implementation issues at the national level (New Zealand Police, 2014). The dashboard was based on four tables:

1. Table 1 determined accountabilities at the district level.
2. Table 2 enabled the police executive to focus on the risks and the issues at the national level.
3. Table 3 measured the reduction in the number of staff during the implementation of the Policing Excellence work streams in the districts.
4. Table 4 (known as the district league table) measures the progress made by the districts in achieving the embedding criteria for each work stream.

## Command Assessments

Command Assessments were a key component of the embedding framework and provided the executive, the Embedding and Realisation Committee, work stream owners, districts and external observers with an assurance that the Policing Excellence program was embedded or was being actively progressed (New Zealand Police, 2014).

Command Assessments were carried out twice in each district between August 2013 and June 2014 (New Zealand Police, 2014). The first Round (CA R1) sought to measure the understanding and the application of the Prevention First program within each of the districts and was guided by the achievement of three objectives:

1. The benchmarking of the depth and breadth of the understanding and uptake of the Policing Excellence program at an area level.
2. The identification of opportunities to sustain the government targets of a 4 percent in the prevention output, a 13 percent decrease in the level of recorded crime and a 19 percent decrease in the number of prosecutions.
3. Policing Excellence is visible and relevant at the area level (New Zealand Police, 2014).

The second assessment round 2 (CA R2) sought to determine the extent to which the districts had satisfactorily embedded the Policing Excellence initiatives and Prevention First. This round was guided by the following three objectives:

- The embedding of the Policing Excellence program is benchmarked across the districts.
- Residual embedding activities are identified.
- The opportunities to sustain the achievement of the three Policing Excellence targets beyond 30 June 2014 are identified (New Zealand Police, 2014).

## Government Level Assessments of Police Performance

In 2009, the State Services Commission, the agency that oversees the New Zealand Government Service, introduced a performance improvement framework, which was based on the United Kingdom's Capability Review Program (State Services Commission, the Treasury and the Department of Prime Minister and Cabinet, 2012). In New Zealand, the Performance Improvement Framework is a term which is used to refer to a review, as well as being an organizational improvement model. The Performance Improvement Framework is used to review an agency's fitness-for-purpose, for both the present and the future, and proposes areas where an agency can improve (State Services Commission, et al., 2012).

The Performance Improvement Framework has two major components: results and organizational management. The results component has two critical areas: delivery of government priorities and the delivery of core business. Organizational management has four critical areas, each of which are supported by a number of elements. The elements are designed to provide a greater level of detail in order to review performance (State Services, et al., 2012). A high-level diagram of the Performance Improvement Framework is presented in Appendix B.

## 2012 Performance Improvement Framework Review of Police

The first Performance Improvement Framework of the police was undertaken in mid-2012 and asked: "What is the contribution that New Zealand needs from the police and therefore what is the performance challenge?" The review reported that if the police were to embed sustainable reductions in crime, road trauma and anti-social behavior through the Prevention First program, then it would need to significantly transform the way that it delivered its services (State Services Commission, et al., 2012). For the police to achieve the objectives outlined in the Policing Excellence program, it needed to focus its attention and efforts in eight critical areas:

1. embedding appropriate financial and performance management systems throughout the organisation;
2. lifting productivity to reallocate resources to more preventative activities;
3. aligning the culture, values and behaviours with the Prevention First Operating Strategy;
4. strengthening people management;
5. implementing knowledge management systems;
6. strengthening strategic partnerships;
7. achieving savings to enable the organization to operate within their budget; and
8. implementing support for IT systems (State Services Commission, et al., 2012).

To achieve the priorities and the outcomes required by the government, the police needed to change their approach to organizational management and emphasize six priority areas:

1. crafting, and rapidly delivering on their consolidated implementation plan;
2. strengthen and align financial and performance management systems;
3. aligning the culture, values and behaviours to strategy;
4. strengthening the management of people;
5. developing a strategic plan and roadmap for the implementation of information systems; and
6. strengthen strategic partnerships (State Services Commission, et al., 2012).

The challenge for the police, according to the State Services Commission, et al. (2012) would be leading and managing the translation of its high-level strategy along with a complex set of new programs and policies into a practical, operational service delivery. Even if done well, it would take a number of years for the strategy to embed and demonstrate its full potential (State Services Commission, et al., 2012).

The Performance Improvement Framework also emphasized that the success of the Prevention First Operating Strategy is intrinsically linked to the successes that other state services agencies achieved. While the police have good relationships with partner agencies and participate in leadership forums across the sector, success will require more collegial relationships. To be successful as a whole, these agencies will need to co-create strategy, prioritise efforts and make difficult trade-offs and shift resources across traditional boundaries (State Services Commission, et al., 2012).

According to the State Services Commission, et al., (2012), the success of implementing the fundamental changes identified in the Prevention First Operating Strategy will depend on:

- An overarching operating model and governance structure that connects individual projects and programs necessary to deliver the strategy.
- An integrated implementation plan with clear milestones, identification of interdependencies, accountabilities, progress monitoring and risk assessment tools.

- Portfolios of projects that have been prioritised and simplified wherever possible to the organisation's deliverables. These projects need to be supported by robust performance measures and exceptional benefit tracking and need to be capable of capturing the effectiveness of expenditure.
- Accountability for delivery of the Prevention First Operating Strategy cascaded through the organisation and monitored by the executive.
- A national resourcing model allowing resources to be extracted, captured and reinvested, where appropriate.
- Financial, asset and risk management having driven improved business performance – business imperatives will form the foundation of annual business plans, budgets and performance targets.
- Centralised support services delivered on time to free up district staff to focus on frontline delivery (State Services Commission, et al., 2012).

## 2014 Performance Improvement Framework Review of Police

The second Performance Improvement Framework, entitled the Follow-up Review, was undertaken in 2014. This review considered whether the police were on track to fulfill its Four-year Excellence Horizon[7]. The overall conclusion from the review was that the Four-year Excellence Horizon remained valid and that the direction the police had developed remained appropriate (State Services Commission, et al., 2014).

The review also noted that the police had performed well during the implementation period of Policing Excellence and Prevention First and that the changes implemented had supported the organization's focus on the five drivers of crime – alcohol, families, youth, road policing, and organized crime and drugs (State Services Commission, et al., 2014). The review also noted that the police were well advanced in being able to meet its three core targets by 30 June 2014; a 13 percent reduction in recorded crime; a 19 percent drop in prosecutions; and a 4 percent increase in prevention activities.

Specifically, the police had made progress in developing an integrated implementation plan to oversee the rollout of Policing Excellence and

[7] The Four year Excellence Horizon helps agencies to understand the changing environment. It is a strategic narrative written for an agency's a senior management team to understand and stay ahead of emerging opportunities and to respond quickly to unexpected issues.

Prevention First, and although they had achieved an improvement in performance as a consequence of the changes, there were still considerable synergy benefits to be realized as the different streams mature and are embedded (State Services Commission, et al., 2014).

### Looking Forward: Embedding Policing Excellence and Prevention First

The 2014 review noted that while a strong platform had been set for the future, there were still a number of areas that required consolidation, continued improvement and ongoing development to embed the Policing Excellence Strategy and Prevention First operating model, including the following:

- The need to identify best practice, and to leverage new capabilities/new development opportunities to further integrate benefits.
- Further develop a more explicit organisational operating model that aligns areas such as workforce strategy, staff performance management, training and development and management/leadership practice.
- Further development the Performance Management Framework, especially in the provision of information to understand what is working and why (State Services Commission, et al., 2014).

## Results from Implementing the 'Prevention First' Strategy

From an examination of Appendix B and Figure 4, it appears that the implementation of the Prevention First Operating Strategy has had an effect on the number of crimes reported, the resolution of crimes and the number of road fatalities. Since the implementation of the 'Policing Excellence' and 'Prevention First' initiatives in 2010, the number of crimes recorded and the number of road fatalities have decreased and the percentage of crimes resolved has remained stable. These outcomes have been achieved while the number of emergency calls for service from the public have increased from 675,708 (1,586 per 100,000 population) in 2008 to 791,662 (1,755 per 100,000 population in 2015), an increase of more than 14 percent, while the number of non-emergency calls for service decreased from 1,385,372 (3,252 per 10,000 population) in 2008, to 1,174,144 (2,603 per 10,000 population) in 2014 (New Zealand Police, 2015), a decrease of more than 15 percent. In addition, public trust and confidence in the police has remained constant at 78 percent of participants surveyed stating that they have full or substantial trust and confidence in the police (Gravitas Research and Strategy, 2009; 2014). Over the same time period, the population of New Zealand has increased by approximately five percent while the ratio of police officers to 100,000 per head of population has remained static.

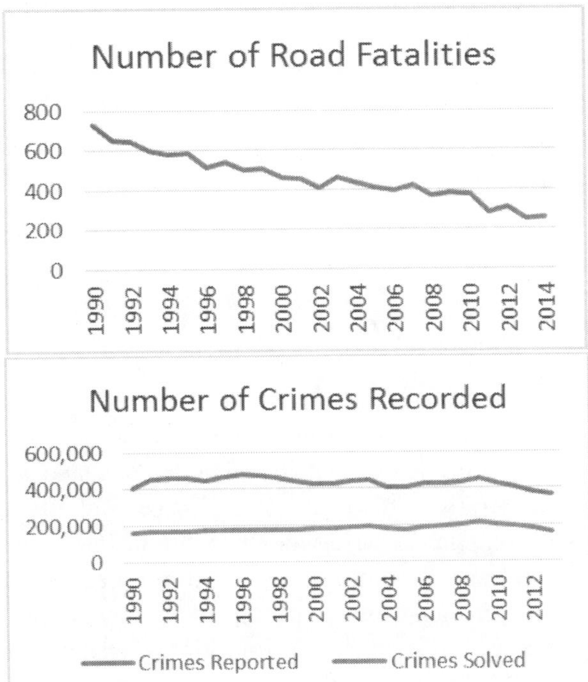


Source: www.statistics.govt.nz.

Figure 4. Number of Road Fatalities, Total Crime and Number of Crimes Resolved from 1990 to 2014.

Furthermore, by 30 June 2014, the three outcome targets set by the government had been achieved as well as:

- a 20.1 percent reduction in recorded crime;
- a 5.8 percent increase in crime prevention activities;
- a 41.3 percent reduction in non-traffic prosecutions;
- the reinvestment of more than 1.2 million hours of frontline officer time, which permitted attention to be increased on the performance of preventative tasks;
- the creation of an additional 214 roles, which focused on crime prevention;
- more effective working arrangements with community groups, volunteers, Iwi and other partners, to develop and implement strategies in the justice, social and transport sectors to reduce crime and victimization and to improve the delivery of services; and
- change to workforce management which released 414,325 hours of frontline activity, which has been reinvested into crime prevention activities and saved the police an estimated $14.9 million in reduced leave accruals between October 2011 and June 2014 (New Zealand Police, 2014).

## CONCLUSION

The 'Policing Excellence' work streams had been designed to enable the police to "become more effective and more focused on prevention" and to be better placed to deal with changing demands (New Zealand Police, 2011a). The aim of the strategy was to facilitate the transfer of officer time from administration and compliance paperwork to working more with the public and with victims, and to preventing problems from escalating (New Zealand Police, 2011a). The strategy was also designed to support the strategies of continuous improvement in external relationships, excellence in leadership, and the development of agency staff (New Zealand Police, 2011c).

A pivotal element which has enabled Policing Excellence and the Prevention First Operating Strategy to succeed has been the Deployment Model[8] (New Zealand Police, 2011b). The comprehensive model was principally designed to deploy staff to manage calls for service, but has enabled the police to deploy staff efficiently and manage demand. The model has four essential components: Critical Command Information, Tasking and Coordination, Workforce Management and Operational Delivery (or

[8] The Deployment Model has often been referred to as the "New Zealand Police Model'.

Execution), which provide up-to-date information and a platform for decision-makers to understand various environmental factors, such as risk.

'Policing Excellence' and 'Prevention First' are both leading police change management programs that have fundamentally changed the way that the police in New Zealand operate and deliver services. These strategies appear to have improved the efficiency of the organization and have influenced the level of reported crime, and have had a notable impact on policing and crime in New Zealand, especially in relation to the increase in preventative policing services. However, to examine the changes that have occurred in policing and in the level of crime, a more structured in-depth analysis needs to be undertaken. 'Policing Excellence' and 'Prevention First' are two innovative police change programs that need to be more thoroughly and systematically evaluated to identify whether they are the methods which will continue to successfully provide the foundation for improving the efficiency and effectiveness of the service delivery of police agencies as they look for alternative means to increase public's trust and confidence.

## References

Cotter, C. (2007). Business process management methodology. Unpublished. Police National Headquarters. Wellington, New Zealand: New Zealand Police.

Gravitas Research and Strategy Limited (2009). *New Zealand Police – Citizens' satisfaction survey: Final report for year two results (July 2008 – June 2009).* Retrieved from the World Wide Web on 17 February 2014 from: http://www.police.govt.nz/sites/default/files/publications/citizen-satisfaction-survey-2009-full.pdf.

Gravitas Research and Strategy Limited (2014). *New Zealand Police – Citizens' satisfaction survey: Final report for 2013/14 fiscal year (July 2013 – June 2014).* Retrieved from the World Wide Web on 24 September 2014 from: http://www.police.govt.nz/sites/default/files/publications/citizen-satisfaction-survey-2014-full.pdf.

New Zealand Police (n.d.). *Tasking and coordination.* Version 1.0. Unpublished. Wellington, New Zealand: New Zealand Police.

New Zealand Police (2009). *Fit for the future project: Executive summary for Police Association.* August. Wellington, New Zealand: New Zealand Police.

New Zealand Police (2011a). *Policing excellence presentation.* 12 October 2011, unpublished, Police National Headquarters, Wellington, New Zealand.

New Zealand Police (2011b). *Prevention First: National operating strategy 2011-2015.* Retrieved on 20 May 2012 from www.police.govt.nz.

New Zealand Police (2011c). *Prevention first: National tactical plan 2013-2014.* Wellington, New Zealand: New Zealand Police.

New Zealand Police (2011d). *The New Zealand police deployment model: Right people, right place, right time, right result: Prevention first – national operating strategy 2011 -2015.* Wellington, New Zealand: New Zealand Police.

New Zealand Police (2012a). *National plan 2012/13 to 2014/15.* Wellington, New Zealand: New Zealand Police.

New Zealand Police (2012b). *Policing excellence presentation.* 9 November 2012, Unpublished, Police National Headquarters. Wellington, New Zealand: New Zealand Police.

New Zealand Police (2013a). *District command centre operating model.* Unpublished, Prevention Group, Police National Headquarters. Wellington, New Zealand: New Zealand Police.

New Zealand Police (2013b). *Drivers of crime: Progress, partnership and opportunities.* Wellington, New Zealand: New Zealand Police.

New Zealand Police (2013c). *Neighbourhood policing team management manual.* Wellington, New Zealand: New Zealand Police.

New Zealand Police (2013d). *Policing excellence: Implementation overview to 30 June 2013.* Retrieved on 5 October 2013 from http://www.police.govt.nz/sites/default/files/publications/policing-excellence-overview-to-30-june-2013.pdf.

New Zealand Police (2013e). *Prevention first: National tactical plan 2013-2014.* Wellington, New Zealand: New Zealand Police.

New Zealand Police (2013f) *Prevention first (tactical assessment).* Unpublished, Police National Headquarters. Wellington, New Zealand: New Zealand Police.

New Zealand Police (2014) *Policing excellence: The transformation of New Zealand police 2009 – 2014.* Wellington, New Zealand: New Zealand Police.

New Zealand Police (2015). *Annual Report 2014-15.* Wellington, New Zealand: New Zealand Police.

Ratcliffe, J. (2004). *Strategic thinking in criminal intelligence.* Annandale, New South Wales, Australia: The Federation Press.

State Services Commission, the Treasury and the Department of Prime Minister and Cabinet (2012). *Performance improvement framework: Formal review of the New Zealand police*. Retrieved on 1 July 2015 from www.police.govt.nz.

State Services Commission, the Treasury and the Department of Prime Minister and Cabinet (2014). *Performance Improvement Framework: Follow-up review of New Zealand Police*. Retrieved on 1 July 2015 from www.police.govt.nz.

## APPENDIX A: THE TACTICAL PLAN IMPLEMENTATION PROCESS

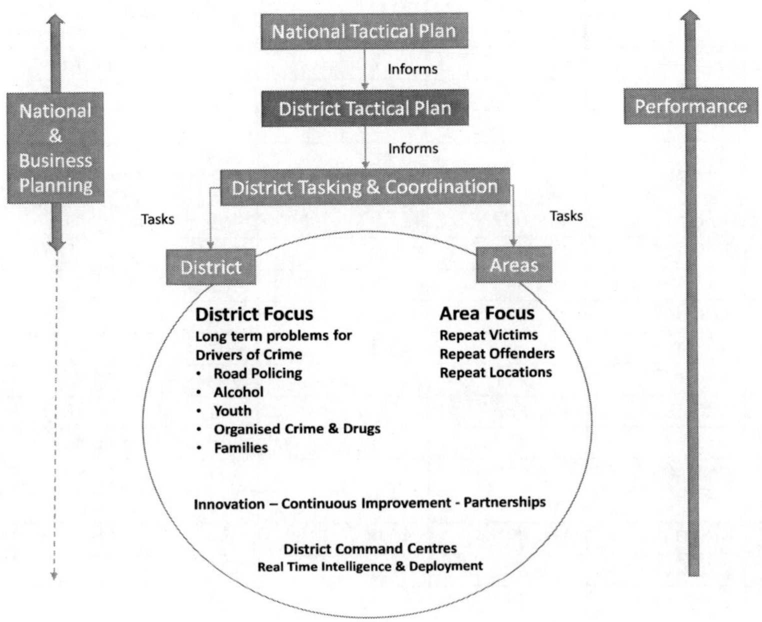


Adapted from New Zealand Police (2011b).

# Appendix B: Level of Reported Crime, Number Resolved, Percentage Resolved, Number of Road Fatalities and Fatalities per 100,000 Population from 1990 to 2013

| Year | Reported Crime | Crime Resolved | Percentage of Crime Resolved | Number of Road Fatalities | Number of Fatalities per 100,000 Population |
|---|---|---|---|---|---|
| 1990 | 405,867 | 161,256 | 39.73 | 729 | 21.4 |
| 1991 | 449,462 | 163,416 | 36.36 | 650 | 18.8 |
| 1992 | 461,523 | 169,873 | 36.83 | 646 | 18.5 |
| 1993 | 458,830 | 167,546 | 36.52 | 600 | 17.0 |
| 1994 | 447,525 | 171,453 | 38.31 | 580 | 16.2 |
| 1995 | 465,052 | 170,649 | 36.69 | 582 | 16.0 |
| 1996 | 477,596 | 175,751 | 36.80 | 514 | 13.8 |
| 1997 | 473,547 | 176,299 | 37.23 | 539 | 14.3 |
| 1998 | 461,677 | 175,176 | 37.94 | 501 | 13.2 |
| 1999 | 438,074 | 170,299 | 38.87 | 509 | 13.4 |
| 2000 | 427,230 | 177,034 | 41.44 | 462 | 21.1 |
| 2001 | 426,526 | 179,007 | 41.97 | 455 | 11.8 |
| 2002 | 440,129 | 184,465 | 41.91 | 405 | 10.3 |
| 2003 | 442,489 | 192,540 | 43.51 | 461 | 11.5 |
| 2004 | 406,363 | 181,344 | 44.63 | 435 | 10.7 |
| 2005 | 407,496 | 176,362 | 43.28 | 405 | 9.9 |
| 2006 | 424,137 | 185,227 | 43.67 | 393 | 9.5 |
| 2007 | 426,384 | 194,768 | 45.68 | 421 | 10.0 |
| 2008 | 431,383 | 201,419 | 46.69 | 366 | 8.6 |
| 2009 | 451,405 | 215,618 | 47.77 | 384 | 8.9 |
| 2010 | 426,345 | 202,545 | 47.51 | 375 | 8.6 |
| 2011 | 406,056 | 190,820 | 46.99 | 284 | 6.4 |
| 2012 | 376,013 | 178,853 | 47.03 | 308 | 6.9 |
| 2013 | 360,411 | 158,042 | 43.85 | 253 | 5.7 |
| 2014 | 350,389 | 145,367 | 41.48 | 254 | 4.4 |

Source: New Zealand Police Annual Reports 1990 to 2014.

## Biographical Sketch

**Name: Garth den Heyer**
Affiliation: Walden University and the Police Foundation
Education: DPubPol, MSS, MSc, BBS.
Address: New Zealand

Research and Professional Experience: Dr. den Heyer is a senior police officer with more than 35 years' service. He is also lecturer with Walden University and is a Senior Research Fellow with the Police Foundation.

**Professional Appointments:**

**Honors:**

**Publications Last 3 Years:**

**Books**

- Prenzler, T. and **den Heyer, G.** (2015). *Civilian Oversight of Police: Advancing Accountability in Law Enforcement.* Boca Raton, Florida: CRC Press.
- **den Heyer, G**. and Das, D. (2014). *Economic development, armed violence and public safety.* Boca Raton, Florida: CRC Press.
- den Heyer, G. (2012). *The role of civilian police in peacekeeping: 1999-2007*. Washington, DC: Police Foundation.

**Chapters**

- den Heyer, G. and Beckley, A. (2015). Police civilian and independent oversight in Australian and New Zealand. In T. Prenzler and G. den Heyer (eds.), *Civilian Police Oversight: Advancing Accountability in Law Enforcement*, Boca Raton, Florida: CRC Press.
- den Heyer, G. (2015). Rainbows across the Mountains? The reform of the Royal Solomon Islands Police Force since 2003. In K. Hope (ed.), *Police Corruption and Police Reform in Developing Societies*, Boca Raton, Florida: CRC Press.

**Peer Reviewed Articles**

- den Heyer, G. (2016). The establishment of Police Scotland: An Analysis of the Reform. *European Journal of Police Studies,* http://www.maklu-online.eu/en/tijdschrift/ejps/online-first/online-first/establishment-police-scotland-analysis-reform/.
- den Heyer, G. (2015). Ghosts of policing strategies past: Is the New Zealand police 'prevention first' strategy historic, contemporary or the future? *Public Organization Review: An International Journal,* (DOI) 10.1007/s11115-015-0323-1.
- den Heyer, G. (2014). Examining police strategic resource allocation in a time of austerity. *Salus Journal*, 2:1, pp. 63-79.
- den Heyer, G. (2013). American policing in an age of austerity and globalization: An option to face the challenge. *Critical Issues in Justice and Politics*, 6:2, pp. 1-26.
- den Heyer, G. (2013). Shape or adapt? The future of policing. *Salus Journal*, 1:1, pp. 41-54.
- den Heyer, G. (2013). Police as nation builders: Distinguishing between countries that contribute police officers to United Nations peace operations. *International Journal of Peacekeeping*, 17: 1-2, pp. 74-115.
- den Heyer, G. (2013). Mayberry revisited: A review of the influence of police paramilitary units on policing. *Policing and Society: An International Journal of Research and Policy.* published online on 15 April and available at http://www.tandfonline.com/doi/pdf/10.1080/10439463.2013.784304.
- den Heyer, G. and Beckley, A. (2013). Police independent oversight in Australian and New Zealand. *Police Practice and Research: An International Journa*l, 14:2, pp. 130-143.

In: Policing
Editor: Jessie Ingram

ISBN: 978-1-63485-369-9


*Chapter 2*

# THE UNIFORM BURDEN: POLICE ACTION DURING WORLD CUP PROTESTS IN BELO HORIZONTE (BRAZIL)

***Débora Rodrigues[1] and Ludmila M. L. Ribeiro[2]***
Center for Crime and Public Safety Studies of Federal University of Minas Gerais, Belo Horizonte, Brazil

## ABSTRACT

In this paper, we analyze the action of the Military Police of Minas Gerais (PMMG) during World Cup protests carried out in 2013 and 2014 in state capital Belo Horizonte. From direct observation of the policing standard adopted in those events, as well as interviews with those responsible for public safety policy, this paper problematizes the excessive use of force, characteristic of military operations, displayed in those moments. The pattern of operation developed by the Military Police during the protests is more characteristic of a war, highlighting the weight of the military uniform as a determinant of police behavior in Belo Horizonte.

[1] Researcher of the Center for Crime and Public Safety Studies (*Centro de Estudos de Criminalidade e Segurança Pública* - CRISP) of UFMG (Federal University of Minas Gerais).

[2] Professor of the Sociology Department and Researcher of the Center for Crime and Public Safety Studies (*Centro de Estudos de Criminalidade e Segurança Pública* - CRISP) of UFMG (Federal University of Minas Gerais).

**Keywords**: public safety, Military Police, World Cup, Brazil

## INTRODUCTION

In June 2013, the Military Police was faced with the task of tackling a previously unseen situation in Brazil: preventing public demonstrations from compromising an international sporting competition. In Belo Horizonte, capital of the State of Minas Gerais, some 100 thousand people took to the streets, as it has happened in several other state capitals around the country.

Said protests were initiated in São Paulo on June 6 that year by the *Movimento Passe Livre* (Free Pass Movement) as a reaction against an increase in municipal public transportation fares. Perhaps due to its violent repression by local Military Police, adding to "the exhaustion of the consumption-based development model promoted by Lulism, the rise of a new middle class with growing demands, and the difficulties faced by President Dilma Rousseff in her first tenure with regard to political articulation" (Sarmento et al., 2015, p. 14), those demonstrations turned from a local phenomenon into a wider movement gaining national representativeness.

By late June 2013, many thousands of people who had never before gone to the streets in order to protest were now engaged in mobilizations, flying various flags and also resorting to *Black Blocks* tactics to attract the attention of the international press. Nonetheless, one of the items in the protesters' agenda was precisely against the immoderate use of force, a stance which "attracted the attention and sympathy of the general public" (Singer, 2013, p. 24). The manifestations did not end in 2013, but triggered a series of new political processes (Sarmento et al., 2015, p. 16) as well as distinct manifestations in the following year, when FIFA World Cup 2014 was hosted by Brazil.

The violent way through which the Military Police of all Brazilian states repressed the 2013 and 2014 protests attracted widespread attention because it directly contrasted with the very nature of the police's mandate – sustained by the idea that they are the sole agent "legally authorized to use force" and, therefore, that "they can interfere by opening up possibilities for conflict resolution that range from negotiations to imposing peaceful forms of obedience" (Muniz et al., 1999, p. 02). We understand that, within a context such as the one shaped by the manifestations arising in connection with FIFA events in Brazil, the use of force might even take place, but without that entailing any violation of rights and, furthermore, without such force being applied with the clear purpose of injuring citizens. Notwithstanding that, the disproportionate use of violence by the Military Police was the rule in all capital cities (rather than the exception, as it should be expected in a Democratic State).

In this paper, we argue that the protests raised in connection with FIFA events in Brazil opened up a window for identifying incongruities in Brazilian democracy: the existence of a Police which is Military not only in its name but also – or especially – in its practice. As an empirical counterpoint, we scrutinized the actions of PMMG (the Military Police of the State of Minas Gerais) during the protests occurred as FIFA events took place in Belo Horizonte, while discussing the measure to which the demobilization tactics employed by that institution may be considered as military in their essence and thus a clear indication of the weight of the regimental uniform worn by the Military Police.

## POLICE IN BRAZIL: INCOMPLETE TRANSITION?

A reality present in our society, the police is the most visible division of public administration and has as its mission maintaining the order within a specified territory, in accordance with the culture of those living in that area. Police history is intertwined with the process of formation of National States and with the assignment of specific powers and duties to their Armies. Despite the function of both institutions being the same, namely, to ensure safety, they differ as to the type of security that is at stake: external or internal.

To ensure external security, the State organizes its Armies with the mission of watching over the borders of its territory (to prevent invasions). To that effect, members of the Armed Forces make use of a wide variety of weapons whose main purpose is to annihilate the enemy and thus put an end to or prevent war. Internal security, on the other hand, is kept by the police forces, whose primary function would be to maintain order and cater for the safety of all individuals and the predictability of daily life in cities. With that in view, Monjardet (2002, p. 293) asserts that "all police is instituted as a force at the service of an order, of a power and its law."

In the early days of their establishment, the police were entrusted with removing wanderers from circulation by means of physical force, while further performing a disciplinary task by reprimanding all those who displayed any deviant behavior in violation of provisions contained in state regulations in general and penal codes in particular (Foucault, 2008). In other words, police arose from the need to control illegalities taking place within the borders of the Nation State, with the mission of regulating coexistence between citizens. It is, therefore, directly connected to the notion of social control. Within this context, it is possible to assert that securing democratic freedom is also a police function. As argued by Soares (2007, p. 07), "there are no liberties without the police, there is no equity or justice without the police. Police forces are fundamental institutions designed to protect rights and liberties." Thus, the police apparatus is seen as an instrument of power (as it represents the State itself), a public service (designed to ensure the safety of citizens, with the keeping of order as the most visible consequence of this corollary) and a profession (to be exercised by specially trained individuals), all at once. In modern societies, this tripod should be harmoniously articulated so that the Police Forces act as instruments to secure democracy itself.

The history of police in Brazil intertwines with the process of establishment and operation of the Nation State itself. According to Bretas and Rosemberg (2013), before the arrival of the Portuguese Court in Brazil (1808), fleeing from Napoleon's armies, the colony relied on local Military Forces in charge of patrolling the urban space, controlling roads and recapturing runaway slaves. However, such bodies could not properly be called 'police,' for they did not fulfill the basic principle of police activity, namely, ensuring collective safety.

The starting point of police activity in Brazil is the arrival of the Portuguese Court, with which all the bureaucratic structure existing in the mother country was recreated in the colony, including its General Police Stewardship (*Intendência Geral de Polícia*), in 1808, just like it existed in Lisbon, and the Royal Police Guard (*Guarda Real de Polícia*), in 1809. The General Police Stewardship – direct predecessor of our present-day Civil Police – was an administrative body with judicial powers in charge of city administration tasks. As for the Royal Police Guard, this was a "body structured similarly to the Army, but having as its main role that of carrying out the mayor's orders in maintaining public peace. From this original Royal Guard there emerged the military-style police forces in uniform that even today perform urban policing in Brazil" (Bretas, 1998, p. 233).

The police organization characteristic of the United Kingdom of Portugal, Brazil and Algarves (1815-1822) was kept without much alteration throughout the imperial period (1822-1889), despite its two compounding institutions being criticized all along for their inability to maintain order and ensure safety from the perspective of citizenry. With the proclamation of the Republic (1889), "the Civil Police had its administrative and judicial functions restricted, while the Military Police would frequently be criticized as unsuited for daily policing, which entailed the creation of other competing police forces in uniform, notably the Civil Guard and the Military Force" (Bretas, 1997, p. 40).

In the first decades of the 20th century, the organization of policing activities was therefore tripartite. There was the Military Force, deployed in case of major collective disorder or uprisings; the Civil Guard, in charge of street policing; and the Civil Police, entrusted with the coordination of city policing and with the investigation of criminal cases. This model persisted for almost eight decades. Then, as Constitutional Amendment no. 1/1967 came to force, (i) the Military Forces were converted into Military Police forces and assigned new prerogatives and duties such as the maintenance of public order, while (ii) the Civil Guards were extinguished and their members incorporated by the Military Police forces. However, "only in 1969 are the Civil Guards merged with the federative states' public forces by means of Decree-Law 667, as amended by Decree-Law no. 1.072/1969, which extinguishes the Civil Guards and institutes the states' Military Police forces (PMs, with the initials in Portuguese) with exclusive competence to conduct ostensible policing (patrolling)" (Fontoura, Rivero and Rodrigues, 2009, p. 139).

Years later, as the Brazilian society shifted from living under a dictatorship (1964-1985) to democracy, national institutions would accordingly be adapted through the enactment of the 1988 Federal Constitution. The 'citizen constitution' – as it became known – provided for fundamental democratic rights and principles, and further included provisions on the organization of powers and states, the defense of states and institutions, economic, financial and social order, direct elections, and more. Nonetheless, the new Constitution did not provide for any changes in the institutional arrangement of police forces as designed during the dictatorship. Thus, the Military Police forces instituted by the Federative States continued to be an auxiliary force to the Army,[3] with powers and duties similar to those that had been assigned to them during the dictatorial period.[4]

Presently, our country is a federation of 27 states, each of which relying in its own Civil Police – in charge of judicial investigatory tasks – and Military

[3] CF/1988 - Art. 144, § 6° - The Military Police forces and military fire brigades, auxiliary and reserve forces of the Army, are subordinate, together with the Civil Police, to the Governors of the States, of the Federal District and of the Territories.

[4] CF/1988 - Art. 144, § 5° - the Military Police forces are charged with ostensible policing and preservation of public order; the military fire brigades are in charge of civil defense activities, in addition to the duties defined by law.

Police. Despite each of the 27 Military Police forces having a differentiated structure of authority, their organization, uniform and operation standards are very similar to those of the Army – the institution from which they originate –, which implies that the use of violence is kept according to standards that would hardly befit the new democratic order.

In fact, human rights violations by the various Military Police started attracting the attention of international bodies such as Amnesty International and Human Rights Watch soon after the transition was completed in 1985. Ever since then, pressure has been exerted in favor of changing the Brazilian police's operational standards to suit the democratic order (Cano, 2006). The problem is, scarce ground has been gained in that regard: as recently as 2014, records indicated that four people were killed everyday by the Military Police in Brazil. In other words, with the transition to democracy, "police institutions, with rare regional exceptions, kept on working as if we lived under a dictatorship or a social apartheid regime" (Soares, 2002, p. 26).

The Military Police of the State of Minas Gerais (PMMG) stands out as an exception from this overall picture of brutality for displaying one of the lowest lethality rates in the country. While in 2014 the combined 27 Brazilian Military Police forces killed as many as 1,576 citizens, the Minas Gerais force (although watching over the country's second largest population) accounted for less than 10% of that total: 99 individuals (FBSP, 2015). While states like São Paulo show a police lethality rate of 1.8 dead in 100,000 inhabitants, the corresponding Minas Gerais rate falls below 0.5. Moreover, in recent decades the institution has sought to introduce changes in its training programs, with focus on new values, beliefs and attitudes to be shared by the organization's elite, while not neglecting nor reducing the time dedicated to disciplines such as firearms handling and urban guerilla tactics, which still take up most of the workload in courses designed to prepare the police for frontline action (Sousa et al., 2009).

In view of the operational style and training structure inherited from the dictatorship, one should only expect that, faced with what the police see as urban chaos, their combat action programs would unfold as if the citizens were enemies of the State. Thus, while demonstrations by the population are legitimate and a natural aspect of political life under democratic rule – particularly in large urban centers where citizens take to the streets to claim rights the State has failed to meet –, for the Military Police of Minas Gerais (PMMG) such argument is not always valid. To the institution, any such demonstration can only be seen as legitimate if certain conditions are duly met: presence of an identified or identifiable leader, no violence, no challenge to the established order. If any of these requirements fail to be met, the police tend to violently repress the protests, which reveals police unpreparedness to deal with demonstrations and the weight of their military uniform.

## Data and Methodology

In this paper, we combined three different sources of information in order to understand how and why PMMG actions during FIFA events in Belo Horizonte can be attributed to the weight of their military uniform. First, we reviewed related official documents, to map the principles guiding the police action prepared for that event. Next, we made direct observations of the interaction between the Military Police and the demonstrators, both in 2013 and 2014, which enabled a more detailed description of the context and subjects involved. Finally, we conducted 25 semi-structured interviews with key actors in local public safety from the following institutions: Military Police (5), Civil Police (5), Federal Police (2), Federal Highway Police (1), Brazilian Intelligence Agency (1), State Secretariat for Social Defense (6), Belo Horizonte City Administration (2), Government of the State of Minas Gerais (2) and FIFA's Local Organizing Committee (1).

In this study, we describe how interactions between PMMG and demonstrators unfolded, and include perceptions of the military police with regard to what such encounters mean in a democratic society. Furthermore, we analyze the extent to which the deployment of war tactics by the institution would symbolize the weight of their uniform – made in the image and likeness to that of the Army.

## Actions Taken by the Military Police of Minas Gerais during FIFA Events

Mega-events bring along with them the need for adequate planning capable of ensuring the tranquility of those who wish to participate in them. In the case of FIFA World Cup, Brazilian public safety bodies were concerned about demonstrations that might take place, given the history of protests occurred in countries that had hosted the event (Rosie and Gorringe, 2009). These phenomena can partially be explained by the greater visibility of the host country to the international press, which makes the event a favorable moment for demands by the local population (Desai and Vahed, 2010). When hosted by South Africa, for example, FIFA World Cup was marked by a series of popular protests in the form of strikes and work stoppages, as means to attract attention to the country's problems – which would not otherwise be taken as object of analysis by the international media (Camargo and Espósito, 2011).

Something of the sort was expected to happen during FIFA Confederations Cup 2013 and FIFA World Cup 2014 in Brazil. Thus, preparation of the Military Police forces in all federative states was initiated in 2010 and jointly conducted with the other local public safety agencies. At the time, a Cup Security Managing Group (GGCopa, with the initials in Portuguese) was created inside SENASP (Brazil's National Secretariat for Public Safety) – a department under the Ministry of Justice (MJ) –, which set the guidelines for police action during the aforementioned events. The GCCopa subsequently became the Special Safety Secretariat for Major Events (SESGE), which – back in 2012 – laid down a specific strategic plan for safety actions to be taken in case of demonstrations. At that point, protests carried a negative connotation, as they were seen as always organized by rioters – which in any case could not be used to justify violent actions by the police, according to this excerpt from the preparatory documents:

> The measures articulated by SESGE/MJ have the following objectives: [...] Implement measures of *systematic action against rioters*; enable the provision of effective public security based on the principles of proportionality, discretion and respect to Human Rights (Brazil, 2012, p. 17 – italics added).

In Minas Gerais, local PMMG set up an advisory group to deal with matters related to the Cup, whose responsibilities included articulation and overall planning of the event – which included the creation of a Cup Battalion comprised of police officers still in training or recently admitted into the force, intended to be deployed during FIFA events in the state capital. This Battalion was designated for actions along two axes: events (tourist places, celebrations, hotels, bus stations, etc.) and demonstrations. As reported by one of the persons in charge of organizing street policing in Belo Horizonte, demonstrations proved to be the Achilles' heel of the entire process:

> Our planning always took that into account, because every international event indeed has *demonstrations*, there's none in the world

> that wouldn't, for there is the group that likes the ball game, that enjoys watching the matches, and there's also the group against it; this is the same anywhere in the world, not only in Brazil, for of course it is a unique opportunity to demonstrate (Interviewee A of the Military Police of Minas Gerais).

Said preparation of the Military Police for the event further included a series of strategic plans, with special focus on the importance of preserving the population's civil rights in the expected scenario of challenges against the established order – such as they tend to happen during FIFA events. The following statement by one of the police officers in charge highlights that dimension:

> Demonstrations were expected. We had evidence that demonstrations might occur, but not at the proportions they actually reached on the days the population adhered. Back in early 2013 or even in 2012 we had evidence pointing at likely demonstrations by professional associations. (...) And this could bring disruptions of public order, of urban mobility, of the citizens' free roaming, all this could be affected. Other entities could join in – I don't want to name names, but there was evidence that some move could be made in that direction, and this actually reached a larger scale and from then on we had to make adaptations in a new planning (Interviewee B of the Military Police of Minas Gerais).

The FIFA event is initiated with the Confederations Cup, which takes place one year before the World Cup and is considered a test event, that is, the moment when the country can demonstrate how well it is prepared (or not) to host the main event. When FIFA Confederations Cup 2013 started, the Military Police forces were astonished to see an explosion of protests in all state capitals. The demonstrations were often arranged via the Internet, and counted many young people (especially university students), but lacked any clear flag defining their points of view or demands.

Until then, the demonstrations that PMMG had experience in dealing with were those staged by unions and social movements, which used to be peaceful (mostly) and previously scheduled and negotiated with the police forces. Hence, there was a dominant sense of perplexity among the ranks, as the police did not know how to respond to that new situation in which a different type of demonstrators brought to the scene an innovative way of organizing the protests:

> The only thing that changed – and I'd say that with all tranquility – was the context, as until then we used to have demonstrations focused on workers' unions and social aspects, while this one had no flag or just the flag of indignation at it all, so the scope was much wider and there was this social commotion, but from that commotion there emerged groups who were neither for nor against the Cup or even the demonstration itself (Interviewee B of the Military Police of Minas Gerais).

Both during FIFA Confederations Cup 2013 and World Cup 2014, demonstrations in Belo Horizonte took place on the days the city hosted the matches – staged in the local stadium popularly known as *Mineirão* and whose official name is *Estádio Governador Magalhães Pinto*. Differences between the two events had to do with the number of people taking part in the protests, the route followed and the tactics employed by PMMG to manage the phenomenon. Nonetheless, in both situations the institution's unpreparedness to deal with the new phenomenon was apparent, as one derives from this statement by another of the interviewees:

> This [the demonstrations] was mapped in our risk analysis, so there was already a perception and a concern about it, but there was no specific preparation to fight that risk. So much so that the level of available equipment reached a critical low during a certain moment. Today there's already a perception, a much greater concern to acquire stun bombs, teargas bombs, pepper sprays, various such things. So, there is today a greater concern for the availability of equipment to counter the demonstrations (Interviewee D of the State Secretariat for Social Defense).

In 2013, thousands of people gathered at the heart of the city – the Praça Sete – and then walked towards the *Mineirão*, and this was the stage for the ensuing clashes between demonstrators and the police, particularly on the 17th, 22nd and 26th of June 2013. In view of what had just happened in São Paulo on June 6, PMMG devised a plan to meet the population's conflicting wishes: those wanting to demonstrate and those wanting to go to the stadium and cheer their team, to properly manage the safety issue involving fans, demonstrators and organizers of the event:

> The original safety plan was changed because it provided for an area of free circulation around Mineirão, for any citizen who did not have tickets [for the games] and we had to set up a new safety scheme to

include an area of restricted circulation around the stadium, because of the demonstrations, to prevent demonstrations from happening next to the stadium (Interviewee A - Belo Horizonte City Administration).

In an attempt to cater for the safety demands of the various segments during FIFA Confederations Cup 2013, the Minas Gerais Governor at the time requested support from the National Force,5 which increased by 150 individuals the Military Police's manpower deployed to restrain the demonstrations. Moreover, another 6000 policemen were dispatched from the state's interior to "reinforce" the capital troops. The General Commander of PMMG at the time said that they had never faced anything like it until then, which would in his opinion justify the transfer of those men to patrol the capital.

> We had never faced a demonstration of this scale. This is unheard of. We have to worry about people's lives. We would not do anything crazy nor embark in any adventure, putting people at risk. Unfortunately, we paid in material damages, but I think the balance is very positive because we didn't pay in lives (PM General Commander Colonel Márcio Sant' Ana, during an interview to Bandnews radio).[6]

In attempting to prevent demonstrations that might render the games unviable, the PMMG's shock troops[7] formed a human barrier around Mineirão, subsequently dubbed 'FIFA perimeter,' and which actually did not coincide with the perimeter defined by the institution for commercial

---

[5] The National Public Security Force (*Força Nacional de Segurança Pública*) was created in 2004 to meet the federative states' emergency needs as to issues requiring a wider intervention from the public authority or where an urgent reinforcement in public security might be necessary. It is formed by the best policemen and firefighters of elite groups from the federative states, who undergo rigorous training at the National Police Academy (of the Federal Police) in Brasilia, which includes a range of topics from crisis management to human rights. In:http://www.justica.gov.br/sua-seguranca/seguranca-publica/forca-nacional, accessed on 08/11/14.

[6] http://www.otempo.com.br/capa/brasil/estrat%C3%A9gia-n%C3%A3o-deve-mudar-1.671882, accessed on 08/11/14.

[7] The Shock Troops (or riot police) are the section of Military Police specialized in controlling large crowds in demonstrations "who are usually euphoric, sometimes requiring the use of methods that go beyond mere verbalization, such as: stun bombs, pepper spray, rubber ammunition shots (anti-riot) and physical force, often applied in self defense or in defense of persons who are unrelated to such demonstrations and who simply wish to have secured their right to come and go or to work, with such police actions being taken in due proportion and solely to the effect of not allowing such disturbances to degenerate into chaos" (Ferreira, 2008).

purposes.[8] Physical barriers were also set up so that even those who resided in the vicinities of the stadium were forced to carry and submit special credentials to gain access to their homes and proximities. That FIFA perimeter was made into an isolated area which one of the interviewees saw as a necessary strategy to ensure safety:

> 'Cause we have 60 thousand people inside the stadium, then I have to preserve the lives of those people, and certainly outside (...) we had nearly 40 thousand people. So I have to preserve the life of both groups. (..) What we have to do as priorities is to make things happen in harmony and obviously to have a beautiful event both for those who come to demonstrate and those inside the stadium (Interviewee E of the Military Police of Minas Gerais).

The means found to achieve "harmony" was to split the city in two pathways for access to *Mineirão*. This division made it possible to observe two different standards of police action on match days. Those accessing *Mineirão* via Presidente Carlos Luz Avenue were spectators of the games who could rely on police services consistent with preservation of life and respect to Human Rights. The other standard was intended for demonstrators who moved along Presidente Antônio Carlos Avenue, the territory where conflicts erupted and where police would indiscriminately use weapons of lesser or greater offensive potential, causing injuries and panic. Such divided city which Belo Horizonte became during FIFA Confederations Cup 2013 was a source of pride to the Military Police, as explained by another interviewee:

> Later on, some people answered what views they had, both people inside the game as well as those in the rallies. What views did they have? Those watching the game did not even know that demonstrations had occurred, that something had happened, and only came to know when they saw it on TV (Interviewee E of the Military Police of Minas Gerais).

As one derives from the statement above, PMMG's action was aimed at holding back demonstrators so that they would not disrupt the sporting event. To that effect, police encirclement of the vicinities around *Mineirão* stadium featured cars, cavalry and policemen shooting rubber bullets, throwing teargas

[8] This measure is intended to prevent companies that are not sponsors of the event from commercially benefitting from it. In that regard, see: http://www.fifa.com/mm/document/affederation/administration/01/84/68/87/areasderestri%C3%A7aocomercial_final.pdf, accessed in March 2014.

bombs and spraying pepper against demonstrators. Even an armored vehicle designed to control gang wars – and popularly known as *caveirão* (big skull)[9] – was used in police operations against the demonstrators. The results from these clashes were numerous injured and the death of two young men who fell off viaduct José de Alencar over Presidente Antônio Carlos Avenue as they fled police repression.

It is important to stress that, in view of the cases of police violence seen in 2013, in the following year the Public Attorney's Office forbid the use of firearms and demanded that the Military Police had an action plan for demonstrations. The Regional Attorney also made recommendations for Citizens' Rights (PRDC), the Federal Attorney's Office (MPF), the Public Attorney's Offices for Human Rights, and the Public Attorney's Office of the State of Minas Gerais (MP-MG) against the use of revolvers and *caveirões* during demonstrations and in favor of a moderate use of weapons of lesser offensive power.[10]

Meanwhile, instructions for police action in Belo Horizonte changed for demonstrations that would occur in connection with FIFA World Cup 2014. The 'envelopment' (or encirclement) tactics used during the 2013 demonstrations in São Paulo – though widely questioned for its restriction of the demonstrators' right to come and go freely – was chosen by PMMG as its main tactics of street action in 2014. Thus, when FIFA World Cup 2014 began, the military police ignored both the judicial orders and the extrajudicial recommendations.

The first resource employed was PMMG's shock troops, mobilized to do the encirclement of demonstrators. This consisted of using helmets and shields to create a security cordon around the demonstrators to prevent them from leaving the circle thus formed. The way such strategy worked during FIFA World Cup 2014 can be better understood by reference to the following statement:

> It was already planned. As the process showed no evolution, the strategy was one of containment. *A complete success*. And there were

[9] To Rebeque et al. (2008), the armored vehicle eerily known as '*Caveirão*' is evidence of a repressive security policy based on confrontation and intimidation strategies and police practices founded on the 'internal enemy logic', and therefore an illustration of the weight of militarism in the police institution.

[10] http://pr-mg.jusbrasil.com.br/noticias/100580162/mps-recomendam-que-orgaos-de-seguranca-evitem-uso-de-armas-nao-letais-nas-manifestacoes-objetivo-e-garantir-a-incolumidade-fisica-dos-manifestantes-e-por-consequencia-a-liberdade-de-reunião, accessed on 25 March 2015.

> also other strategies for further developments, but there's nothing to say [...] first it was an action more intended to halt the process, insofar as this is possible, and this was decisive to avoid vandalism. And there was also a second and good point: as the police did the containment no demonstration could take place any longer. The tactics adopted, the strategy adopted really worked and it was a comprehensive success 'cause obviously it was appropriate for that sort of demonstration of larger proportions, which could also entail other strategies – but this was not necessary (Interviewee D of the Military Police of Minas Gerais).

During FIFA World Cup 2014, protests where contained at their points of origin, such as Savassi, Sete and Terminal squares – Belo Horizonte's three main central plazas. Minas Gerais' justice authority considered those 'enveloping' actions as abusive and issued an injunction forbidding the use of such tactics. The injunction was soon revoked,[11] and PMMG proceeded to use them freely in the following days. As the demonstrations did not achieve the expected scale – for the young demonstrators of 2013 were now (in 2014) enjoying the World Cup events –, the 'envelopment' was considered as the most effective tactics from the point of policing during demonstrations, for having prevented them from spreading around the city:

> So, within the context, it worked very well as intended. We aimed at the maximum, the worst that could happen, but we gained control and everything went calmly. Our top concern – the public demonstrations – did not have a big impact, as they were controlled in the dimension they had (Interviewee C of the Military Police of Minas Gerais).

Still as part of the strategy for action adopted by local public safety agencies, more emphasis was placed on procedures followed by the judiciary police, differently from what had happened in 2013 – when the Military Police was the main protagonist and violently repressed the demonstrators. One single Civil Police station, of the several existing in the city, was chosen to receive the entire flow of detainees brought over by PMMG, with the purpose of gaining agility and centralizing the process of recording police incidents. This decision was agreed and articulated between the Public Attorney's Office, the Office of the Public Defender, the Police (military and civil) and the Judiciary. However, even with this new tactics, there were reports of

[11] http://amp-mg.jusbrasil.com.br/noticias/125334690/liminar-que-proibia-cerco-da-pm-em-manifestacoes-e-cassada-pela-justica, accessed on 10/08/2014.

detainees being taken to other posts, in disagreement with what had been previously established. Furthermore, the first day of event saw the arbitrary arrest of demonstrators who would only be released after the end of FIFA World Cup 2014, which prevented mobilization tactics to be employed by more engaged leaders. Clearly, there was arbitrariness in conducting this process.

It is interesting to note that, according to Minas Gerais Civil Police, most of those detainees had criminal records for theft, robbery and drug trafficking, which seems to indicate that the organizations in charge of providing public safety took advantage of the protests to make arrests that had no legal backing whatsoever. Otherwise, how to explain that only "*bandidos*" were arrested during police operations aimed at managing the demonstrators' excesses?

As the 2014 football games came to a close in Belo Horizonte, police actions taken during the event were questioned by Human Rights entities for not having followed UN guidelines contained in the Universal Declaration on Human Rights, on how authorities should proceed in face of public demonstrations: peacefully, that is, without recourse to war tactics (such as the aforementioned 'envelopment') or, even less so, weapons such as teargas spray and rubber bullets, not to mention highly lethal ones (such as the '*caveirão*' and firearms). PMMG was also questioned relatively to breaches represented by arbitrary arrest of demonstrators, by the deployment of non-identified law enforcement agents and by the lack of a negotiation protocol.

Therefore, the data reviewed indicate that during FIFA events occurred in 2013 and 2014 in Belo Horizonte, the Military Police acted as an auxiliary force of the Army, using excessive force rather than otherwise handling the demonstrations. Policing standards consistent with Human Rights principles were only adopted to deal with visitors (tourists) or with those wishing to enjoy the related events. The remainder was treated with the excessive violence of actions structured to hinder the exercise of the basic right to come and go freely. This operation standard renders apparent the weight of the military uniform. When PMs (i.e., military police) are called upon to act in face of movements that are typical of a democratic order (such as protests and demonstrations) they end up resorting to war tactics – which may be consistent with their uniform, but not with the idea of policing in a free society.

## DISCUSSION

In a democracy, the key indicator of success for a police institution is its ability to reconcile respect for individual rights and liberties with preservation of public order and safety. The right to free manifestation is inherent to the very idea of a Democratic State, and it can and should be exercised by the citizens. Appropriately policing manifestations is crucial for democracy to thrive, for the police represent the more immediate institution of the State, and their strategies for keeping order will influence the population's perception of the state's power practices – including the extent to which individual rights and liberties are respected.

Legislation in force in Brazil recognizes the right to free manifestation as the foundation of democracy itself, and sees the State as its guardian. This includes: the 1988 Federal Constitution,[12] the Universal Declaration of Human Rights (signed by Brazil on 10 December 1948),[13] the UN International Covenant on Civil and Political Rights (ratified in Brazil by Decree 592 of 1992),[14] and the Interamerican Convention on Human Rights (signed by Brazil on 07/09/92).[15] These documents stress that the police shall protect and facilitate public demonstrations by adopting premises such as communication, cooperation, information, negotiation and implementation of preventive actions.

Given its constitutional duty to perform ostensible policing, the Military Police should be ready to act in face of popular protests, to keep public order, but also, and above all, to secure their unimpeded right to manifestation and assembly – in especial those of an ideological nature. To that effect, the institution should apply the Negotiated Management principle that instructs

[12] Art. 5º IV – expression of thought is free, with anonymity being forbidden; XVI – everyone may gather peacefully, not bearing arms, in places open to the public, regardless of authorization, provided they do not frustrate any other meeting previously summoned to that same site, with the only requirement being prior notice to the competent authority.

[13] Art. 19 Every person has the right to freedom of opinion and expression; this right includes the freedom to unimpededly entertain opinions and seek, receive and convey information and ideas by any means and regardless of borders.

[14] Art. 19, §1. No one shall be molested for their opinions. §2. Everyone shall have the right to freedom of expression; this right shall include the right to seek, receive and disseminate information and ideas of any nature, regardless of border considerations, either orally or in writing, in print or artistic form, or by any other means of their choosing.

[15] Art. 15 – Right to assemble – The right to assemble peacefully and without weapons is hereby acknowledged. The exercise of such right shall only be subject to the restrictions provided for under the law and as made necessary, in a democratic society, to the interest of national security, public security and order, or to protect public health or morals, or the rights and liberties of the others.

the police not to take position *against* demonstrators, while stressing that the Police should, rather, cooperate with them so that the protests unfold peacefully. Nonetheless, as seen in the previous section hereof, the military police's standard approach to the demonstrations staged in Belo Horizonte during FIFA Confederations Cup 2013 and World Cup 2014 was very different from what should be expected.

During FIFA Confederations Cup 2013, the less lethal weapons mostly used by PMMG were stun bombs, batons, pepper spray, teargas bombs and rubber bullets. In many – if not all – cases, there was no respect for standards set under national and international protocols as to progressive use of force, and many people resulted injured in vital parts of the body (like head and chest). Teargas bombs were thrown amidst the crowd without there being any shelter where they could protect themselves – as guidelines would have it. Moreover, weapons of high offensive potential – such as revolver shots and the '*caveirão*' – were also employed to disperse the demonstrators.

PMMG was intent to thwart demonstrations scheduled for FIFA World Cup 2014 by using disproportionate force, both in the form of an overwhelming number of police officers and of crowd encirclement by shock troops with shields, dark uniforms, batons and weapons deployed around demonstrators, thus conveying the message that they were ready to severely curtail any disorder. Furthermore, arbitrary arrests legitimated by local Civil Police resulted in restrictions of the right to roam of several citizens, simply because they seem to "look like a demonstrator."[16] Evidently, the institution aimed at keeping the demonstrators away from areas where they might disrupt the event, be it in the vicinities of *Mineirão*, in squares around the city where fans were concentrated, or at strategic points and circulation routes, thus revealing the face of a police organization ready to use force to coerce anyone who goes against their interests.

However, both in 2013 and 2014, in the surroundings of stadiums and *fan fest*[17] points, one could verify the existence of another police, with standards of action and service rather in keeping with the principles of a Democratic State under the Rule of Law. Such was the case of the police force put at the service of tourists/fans, made up of friendly and helpful officers, of agents that secured the safety of those who were there to take part in FIFA events.

The events witnessed in the Minas Gerais capital endorse the image of a militarized police force that will act differently under different circumstances,

---

[16] Literal words of one of the interviewees in our survey.

[17] According to Viol (2009), "*FanFest* is the name given by FIFA to the gathering of population in public squares to watch the football games on large screens".

in accordance with their understanding of how should police behave in face of each 'type' of citizen. Instead of protecting the citizens who were in the streets exercising their right to free manifestation, secured by the 1988 Federal Constitution, PMMG acted to ensure that FIFA events happened without any disturbances to those who paid large sums for tickets to the matches in *Mineirão*. To that effect, it even resorted to force – in disregard for the limits set by national decrees and international covenants. In short, what we verified in these cases was an extensive use of force with the objective of showing to demonstrators the institution's military power.

Historical studies on standards of police action demonstrate that the excesses incurred by PMMG during FIFA mega-events in Belo Horizonte originate from a police culture that stresses a war against the internal enemy – who could only be won over by employing force. This way of acting reveals the weight of the uniform still carried by the Military Police of Minas Gerais. When members of this institution find themselves faced with the difficult mission of protecting diverse individuals, they still choose to protect the elites and governmental interests, as if the country was still under a dictatorship that must annihilate all those contrary to the prevailing ideology. Massacring demonstrators by applying excess lethal force and 'envelopment' is to give unequivocal evidence that PMMG's policing standard is essentially as military as their uniform.

## FINAL CONSIDERATIONS

The intention of this paper was to provide a panorama of actions taken by the Military Police of Minas Gerais in face of demonstrations occurred in Belo Horizonte during FIFA Confederations Cup 2013 and World Cup 2014, with a view to discussing the manner by which the actions engendered by said institution carry military nuances that are scarcely consistent with the principles of a Democratic State.

The data collected from direct observation, document analysis and semi-structured interviews indicate that the Military Police of Minas Gerais acted to prevent popular demonstrations from compromising FIFA events of 2013 and 2014. With that purpose, the institution resorted to excessively military actions, leaving aside national and international standards and guidelines regulating the use of force by police, in addition to fundamentals of Brazil's federal constitution. In contrast, PMMG's attitude towards those whose had tickets for the mega-events was rather differentiated and respectful, thus indicating that the progressive use of force is calibrated according to the profile of the citizen with whom the police interact.

Therefore, the demonstrations discussed herein exposed the facet of a police force that carry in their uniform a model of action that evokes and replicates military institutions such as the Army, thus revealing how the Military Police adopt an attitude of combat and elimination of the enemy, as if they were in a war. Thus, even as their action should be guided by principles consistent with the Democratic State under the Rule of Law, the weight of their uniform tilts the balance in the opposite direction. The episodes described may be seen as a sign of the pressing need to reform the Military Police, to turn it into an institution whose role is not a repressive but rather a preventive one, capable of promoting everyone's safety and the respect for all citizens' rights and not only those of the elites.

## Funding

This work has been developed with financial support from CNPq (Brazil's National Council for Scientific and Technological Development) – aid no. 400049/2013 -9.

## References

Brasil. Ministério da Justiça. Secretaria Extraordinária de Segurança para Grandes Eventos. Planejamento estratégico de segurança para a Copa do Mundo FIFA Brasil 2014 (2010). Brasília, 2012. Disponível em: <http://blog.justica.gov.br/inicio/wp-content/uploads/2012/11/ PROGRAMAÇÃO-OFICIALDA-CONFERÊNCIA-SISGE.pdf>. Acesso em: 18 ago. 2013.

Bretas, Marco Luiz. A Polícia carioca no Império. Revista Estudos Históricos, v. 12, n. 22, p. 219-234, 1998.

Bretas, Marcos Luiz; Rosemberg, André. A história da polícia no Brasil: balanço e perspectivas. Topoi (Rio de Janeiro), v. 14, n. 26, p. 162-173, 2013.

Bretas, Marcos Luiz. Observações sobre a falência dos modelos policiais. Tempo Social, v. 9, n. 1, p. 79-94, 1997.

Camargo, Carlos Alberto de. Espósito, Eduardo. Um estudo de Caso. "Estudo sobre a copa do mundo de futebol FIFA 2010 realizada na África do sul e as lições para a organização da Copa no Brasil." São Paulo: disponível em: http://visaoconsultores.com.br/2013/03/25/estudo-grandes-eventos-africa-do-sul/, acesso em março de 2015.

Cano, Ignacio. Políticas de segurança pública no Brasil: tentativas de modernização e democratização versus a guerra contra o crime. Sur. Revista Internacional de Direitos Humanos, v. 3, n. 5, p. 136-155, 2006.

Desai, Ashwin; VaheD, Goolam. World Cup 2010: Africa's turn or the turn on Africa?. Soccer & Society, v. 11, n. 1-2, p. 154-167, 2010.

FBSP. 9º. Anuário do Fórum Brasileiro de Segurança Pública. São Paulo: Fórum Brasileiro de Segurança Pública, 2015.

Ferreira, Aldo Bruno. Tropas de Choque e os Direitos Humanos. (Especialização) – PRONASCI/ULBRA, Canoas, 2008.

Fontoura, Natália de Oliveira; Rivero, Patricia Silveira; Rodrigues, Rute Imanishi. Segurança Pública na Constituição Federal de 1988: continuidades e perspectivas. Brasília: Instituto de Pesquisa Econômica Aplicada, 2009.

Foucault, Michel. Segurança, Território e População, São Paulo, Martins Fontes, 2008.

Monjardet, Dominique. O que faz a Polícia: sociologia da Força Publica; posfácio Jean-Marc Erbès; tradução Mary Amazonas Leite de Barros. – ed. Ver. 2002 – São Paulo: Editora da Universidade de São Paulo, 2003.

Muniz, Jacqueline et al. "Uso da força e ostensividade na ação policial." Conjuntura Política: boletim de análise, n. 6, p. 22-26, 1999.

Paula, Marilene de. Copa para quem e para quê? Um olhar sobre os legados dos mundiais de futebol no Brasil, África do Sul e Alemanha. Marilene de Paula, Dawid Danilo Bartelt (organizadores). – Rio de Janeiro: Fundação Heinrich Böll, 2014.

Rebeque, Cristiano; JAGEL, Daniela Couto; BICALHO, Pedro Paulo Gastalho. Psicologia e políticas de segurança pública: o analisador 'Caveirão.' Psico, v. 39, n. 4, 2009.

Rosie, Michael; Gorringe, Hugo. 'The Anarchists' World Cup': Respectable Protest and Media Panics. Social Movement Studies, v. 8, n. 1, p. 35-53, 2009.

Sarmento, Rayza; REIS, Stephanie; Mendonça, Ricardo Fabrino. As Jornadas de Junho e as questões de gênero: as idas e vindas das lutas por justiça. PUC-Rio: compolítica, 2015.

Singer, André. Brasil, junho de 2013, classes e ideologias cruzadas. Novos Estudos-CEBRAP, n. 97, p. 23-40, 2013.

Soares, Luiz Eduardo. "A polícia do Futuro: A força policial é a única das instituições que não foi retomada após o fim da ditadura." In: Super Interessante especial segurança: Por um Brasil menos violento. Ed. Abril de 2002 (a), p.26.

Soares, Luiz Eduardo. Pressupostos, razões e condições para uma reforma das polícias brasileiras. Ratton, JL; Barros, M. Polícia, democracia e sociedade. Rio de Janeiro: Editora Lúmen Júris, 2007.

Sousa, Eros Soares; Couto, Vinícius; Ribeiro, Ludmila. As políticas de segurança pública pensadas para a Copa do Mundo de 2014 podem garantir os Direitos Humanos?. In: VIII Encontro da Andhep, 2014, São Paulo. Anais do VIII Encontro da Andhep. São Paulo: Andhep, 2014. v. 1. p. 3162-3184.

In: Policing
Editor: Jessie Ingram
ISBN: 978-1-63485-369-9


*Chapter 3*

# POLICING CYBER TERRORISM IN AFRICA: PERSPECTIVES, PROBLEMS AND PROSPECTS

***Philip N. Ndubueze**, PhD***
Department of Sociology
Federal University Dutse, Jigawa State, Nigeria

## ABSTRACT

Terrorists' use of internet infrastructure for the advancement of their agendas is an emerging problem that has elicited serious global concern. Critical national infrastructure such as electricity generation, telecommunications, transportation systems, financial services, gas/oil production, emergency and security services are increasingly depending on computer networks and are now vulnerable to attack by terrorist organizations. However, most researches on terrorism have tended to focus on traditional classical, real world terrorism, while cyber terrorism is relegated to the background culminating in a dearth of research in the area. This chapter attempts to bridge that gap by critically examining the emerging problem of cyber terrorism. The chapter x-rays the concept of cyber terrorism as well as the tenor of existing scholarship on how to police it. It discusses the scope and ramifications of the problem and proposes a model for effectively policing Africa's terror-genic cyberspace. The proposed policing strategy may work for countries faced

* E-mail: pnndubueze@gmail.com

with the growing threat of cyber terrorism who share similar demographics with developing countries of Africa.

## INTRODUCTION

Societies across the world are undergoing rapid and unprecedented transition. The metamorphoses from the physical space to the cyber space. This transition permits every stratum and sector of the twenty-first century global economy. Hitherto analog systems and processes are increasingly digitalized and virtualized. Virtual borders are relatively open, porous, under-policed and unregulated. They are not characterized by perimeter barbed-wire fences, surveillance cameras, bomb detectors and anti-bomb police squads. The cyber space is bugged by a congregation of computers, sometimes, with ill-updated/obsolete anti-virus and anti-spy tools kits. Conceptually, illicit and unlawful activities on the cyber space would primarily fall under three broad categories namely: cyber deviance, cybercrime and cyber terrorism. Cyber deviance would include those minor infractions and nuisances that are not criminalized by the state such as adult private pornography viewing, use of vulgar language in social media chat rooms or informal e-mail communications, cyber loitering etc. Cybercrime generally include all online activities prohibited and punishable by the state like online advance fee fraud commonly referred to as 'yahoo-yahoo' in Nigeria, cyber stalking, online identity theft etc. Cyber terrorism would include any unlawful online activity that is aimed at disrupting critical infrastructure or any computer network on a large scale, with a view to coercing, intimidating, embarrassing, distracting or discrediting the government or a group with a view to scoring some cherished political, religious, ideological, national, or regional points. It may also include any online propaganda or activity by individuals or a group that is aimed at discrediting, malingering, slandering or coercing the government.

African has a lingering terrorist problem. The Symatec Report (as cited in United Nations Economic Commission of Africa, 2014) indicates that in 2014 the number of targeted cyber-attacks in Africa increased by 42 per cent and that thirty-one per cent of these attacks regarded as cyberespionage affected both large and small businesses. It further observes that in major African cities, such as Cairo, Johannesburg, Lagos and Nairobi, the rate of cyber-related offences such as fraudulent financial transactions and child trafficking particularly in Kenya has doubled in the past three years. It is therefore safe to argue that threat of cyber terrorism is real and the potential scope of its outcome could be ridiculously sweeping. Although, unlike classical terrorism, cyber terrorism has not generated moral panic in Africa and as such has not received serious media attention in Africa.

*"Cyber terrorism and cyber-crime are on the rise... almost all observers, with rare exception, share this view"* (Gori, 2009, p. vii). Terrorists are increasingly aware and interested in the Internet (Denning, cited in Rogers, 2003). Critical national infrastructure such as electricity generation, telecommunications, transportation systems, financial services, gas/oil production, emergency and security services are increasingly depending on computer networks and are now vulnerable to attack by terrorist organizations. However, most researches on terrorism have tended to focus on traditional (classical), real world terrorism, while cyber terrorism is relegated to the background culminating in a dearth of scientific research in the area especially in Africa. This chapter attempts to bridge that gap by critically x-raying the concept of cyber terrorism as well as the breath of existing scholarship on how to police it. It discusses the scope and ramifications of the emerging problem and proposes a model for effectively policing Africa's terror-genic cyberspace. Nonetheless, the proposed policing strategy is considered workable for countries faced with the growing threat of cyber terrorism who share similar demographics with developing countries of Africa.

## Basic Concepts

Terrorism, Cyber Terrorism, Policing and Space Transition are the basic concepts that need to be clarified in this discourse.

## Terrorism

Many scholars and researchers contend that defining the concept of terrorism is a difficult task and so is the quest for a generally acceptable definition of the term (see, Eruvebetine, 2008; Gibbs, 1989, Goodwin, 2006; Lequueur, 1977, Onapaju, Uzodike & Whetho, 2012). Terrorism can be understood at individual and group level (Crenshew, 1990) but historically connotes: "acts of physical violence, such as bombings, kidnappings, murder and other atrocious crimes, to send a political message" (Marcum, 2014, p. 132). Waugh (2001) identifies key concepts of terrorism as follows:

a. The use of threats or usual violence.
b. Goal-focused and intent to cause harm.
c. Intent to psychologically disorganize and horrify their main victims as well as those around them.
d. Victims are chosen for their symbolic value.

Terrorism is said to have some similarities with guerilla warfare. Guerilla warfare have been described as asymmetric and entailing a situation where a party has more technological advantage over the other, thereby making the weaker party resort to unconventional tactics and different behavior in response to the situation and conditions (Heickerb, 2014). Moreover, it should be noted that terrorism is not just a lone, group or organizational affair. State actors may for certain political, security or hegemonic reasons carry out cyber-attacks. Roscini (2014) points out that cyber operations executed by states may include cyber-attack and cyber exploitation.

## Cyber Terrorism

The word "Cyber Terrorism" was coined by Barry Collin in 1997 (Marcum, 2014). Cyber terrorism, has been defined as "the use of computer network tools to harm or shutdown critical national infrastructure (such as energy, transportation, government operations)" (Weimann, 2005). "Despite copious media attention, there is no consensus methodology by which various actions may be placed under the nomenclature 'cyber terrorism, yet the term clearly exists in common usage' (Hamben, Leing as cited in Gordon & Ford, 2003, p. 3). Denning (2000, n.p) captures the nature of cyber terrorism while testifying before the Special Oversight Panel on Terrorism in the United States of America thus:

> Cyberterrorism is the convergence of terrorism and cyberspace. It is generally understood to mean unlawful attacks and threat against computers, networks, and the information stored therein when done to intimidate or coerce a government or its people in furtherance of political or social objectives. Further, to qualify as cyber terrorism, an attack should result in violence against persons or property, or at least cause enough harm to generate fear. Attacks that lead to death or bodily injury, explosions, plane crashes, water contamination, or severe economic loss would be examples. Serious attacks against critical infrastructures could

be acts of cyber terrorism, depending on their impact. Attacks that disrupt non-essential services or that are mainly a costly nuisance would not.

Clearly, Denning's elaborate definition of cyber terrorism highlights the key elements of cyber terrorism and distinguishes it from other forms of criminality perpetrated on the cyber space. Fundamentally, cyber terrorism will include the following critical elements:

a) The act must be committed using the Internet as a medium.
b) The motive for committing the act must be political, social, ideological, religious, ethnic, national or regional.
c) It must cause bodily/virtual harm, death or large scale disruption of computer system/network or critical infrastructure.
d) It must create some kind of fear or apprehension on the primary (direct victims) or the secondary victims (their family, friends and colleagues).
e) The act must embarrass the government and its agencies.
f) It must be serious enough to elicit media attention and public reaction. In other words it must create moral panic.

It is important to note that scholars have also identified a variant of cyber terrorism known as "Pure Cyberterriosm," which describes terrorism activities that occur entirely or basically in the virtual world (see, Gordon & Ford, 2003). There is difference between 'pure' cyber terrorists and terrorists who use the internet to coordinate attacks. The former hides his intentions until he carries out a full-scale info logical attack and considers cyber terrorism as a safe, profitable and less detectable option (Heickerb, 2014).

## Policing

The term "police" is said to have originated from the Latin word "politia" which means "civil administration" (Dempsey & Frost, 2008). It has been argued that police officers of the political era were more concerned about regulating criminal activity than policing it (Worrall & Schmalleger, 2016). Policing the cyber space compounds the already challenging police work in the twenty-first century. Thus, it is believed that police units lack adequate capacity and knowledge of and experience with cyber-crime cases and do not consider the impact of cyber cases as significant as traditional cases

(Leukfeldt, Veenstra & Stool, 2013). Policing must be tailored to fit the dynamics of the cyber world for it to be effective (Ndubueze & Igbo, 2014).

## Space Transition

According to Wentz (2011) the term cyber includes aspects of information and information communication technology (ICT). Space transition is used here to refer to the migration from the physical, real world platform to the abstract virtual space platform. There is a massive migration going on Africa, albeit covet but monumental in the space. Hitherto analogue and manual systems and now digitalized making the acquisition of Internet skill set mandatory for the average African. Obviously, those who cannot fit in into the growing digital culture will have a hard time doing business and pursuing tertiary education in Africa. Besides, they will be among the most vulnerable as they will depend on third parties such as trusted family members and friends or broker business agents to do their online transaction. These third parties (if criminally-minded) may exploit their naivety to defraud them of their hard earned monies or use their online identity to perpetrate criminal activities. The African digital natives (those born during internet boom) are space-transition compliant, while their counterparts, the digital-immigrants (who were born before the internet boom) are made up of a mixture of those who are space-transition complaint as well as those who have Internet-phobia and are struggling with this transition. Expectedly, in Africa, the space transition is progressing at a geometric rate, of course with deep seated implications for parenting, privacy, policy making and cyber security and law enforcement.

## Crime and Terrorism: A Conceptual Clarification

Generally speaking, crime and terrorism fall under the purview of felonies and criminality. However, by their very nature and objective they essentially constitute different forms of criminality. Although, experts have tried to draw a line between crime and terrorism, nonetheless, these lines are often thin and sometimes blurred. The distinguishing element between crime and terrorism is perhaps the motivation/goal and targets. The table below illustrates this point more aptly.

**Table 2. Distinction between Cyber Crime and Cyber Terrorism**

| Attribute | Cyber Crime | Cyber Terrorism |
|---|---|---|
| Motivation/ Objective | Sheer demonstration cyber-ingenuity/wizardry. Steal sensitive information, pursue criminal gains/ends. | Coerce, embarrass, intimidate and discredit the government, harm targeted individuals/groups/organization, court media publicity. |
| Perpetrators | Hackers, criminals | Terrorists |
| Victims | Individuals, groups and organizations. | Individuals, government agencies and organizations/groups (political, religious, racial or ethnic). |
| Motivation | Deviance and criminal-oriented | Politically, socially, religiously, racially or ethnically-motivated |

Basically, the hallmark of terrorism as opposed to crime is the motive and structure. The former is politically, ideological, religiously, ethnically, nationally or regionally motivated, while the latter is not. The former is usually orchestrated by insurgent and extremist groups, while the latter is often perpetrated by a criminal subculture, gang or organization. The former is not often pecuniary-oriented, while the latter for the most part is. Above all, in the former the offender may consciously sacrifice his/her life, while in the latter it would be rare and absolutely strange to do so.

The distinction between classical terrorism and cyber terrorism can be depicted in sphere, target, scope, territory and speed the table below.

## Theoretical Framework

Several theories have been used by scholars and researchers to explain the different kinds of illegal and disorderly activities that are carried out in the cyber space. Our current discourse is explained within the framework of the Routine Activity Theory (RAT).

**Table 1. Attributes of Classical and Cyber Terrorism – A Comparative Snapshot**

| Attribute | Classical Terrorism | Cyber Terrorism |
|---|---|---|
| Motivation/Objective | Political, religious, social, national, ethnic, ideological and hegemonic. | Political, religious, social, national, ethnic, ideological and hegemonic [essentaiily the same motivation with classical terrorism]. |
| Sphere | Physical, real world, offline, concrete space. | Cyber, virtual, online abstract space. |
| Primary Target | Humans, property, physical critical infrastructure | Computer systems/networks/ computer mediated communication systems, internet architecture/internet of things, virtual critical infrastructure |
| Scope | Limited to a select and relatively small physical targets. | Massive, large scale virtual targets. |
| Territory | Select countries | Several countries |
| Execution Speed | Minutes/Hours | Seconds |
| Modus Operandi | Overt, physical contact with or close proximity to the target (s). Suicide bombing. | Covert, virtual contact with and unlikely close proximity with the target. |
| Tools | Fire-arms/ammunitions of all sorts, rocket launchers, IED's, grenades, armored tanks, machine guns and so on. | Malwares of all sorts. |
| Nature of Warfare | Asymmetric, guerrilla warfare | Asymmetric |
| Detection | Swift | Slow |
| Economic Loss | Huge | Incredibly massive and high |
| Investigation | Traditional, regular law enforcement/anti-terrorism personnel could be used. | Technical, requires highly trained/skilled and experienced law enforcement personnel including forensic experts, cyber criminologists and experts in international |

## Routine Activity Theory (RAT)

The Routine Activity Theory (RAT) is associated with the works of Cohen and Felson (1979) and Clarke and Felson (1993). According to RAT three elements are required for crime to occur. A motivated offender must meet a suitable target where a capable guardian is absent. Suitable targets are viewed with reference to the benefits of the crime and may include a person, an object or a place. Conversely, capable guardians are considered with reference to the costs of the crime and may include neighbors, property owners, and the police. The last element is the presence of a motivated offender: someone who is incentivized to commit crime because of the perception of a potentials target (such as an expensive jewelry) as suitable. According to RAT, crime will only occur if a motivated offender thinks that a target is suitable and a capable guardian absent (Clarke & Felson, 1993; Felson & Clarke, 1998; Felson,1998). The theory further argues that the supply of suitable targets and the presence of capable guardians are a function of people's routine activities such as family, work, leisure, consumption as so on. Therefore, an upsurge in crime may be as a result of changes in the normal life-style of people rather than the emergence of pathological social conditions (Cullen, Agenw & Wilcox, 2014).

Tittle (as cited in Cullen, Agenw & Wilcox, 2014) have criticized RAT for not specifying which of our routine activities are best suited for the explanation of crime. Similarly, the theory has been criticized for not explaining the factor that influences the offender's decision to commit crime (Adler & Laufer, 1998).

The Routine Activity Theory (RAT) is useful in the understanding of cyber terrorism. Cyber terrorism is usually an outcome of perceived marginalization is society, a scenario that creates the motivated offender mentioned in RAT. People who reside in terror-prone environments and critical infrastructure are suitable targets and may be attacked if not guarded by a capable guardian. Similarly, the cyber space gives terrorists a platform to recruits members from any part of the world, train and deploys them. Besides, it also gives terrorists the leverage to launch attacks in ways that would not be possible in the physical space.

## Terrorism and Space Transition: From Physical to Cyber Domain

Each phase of societal development has been characterized by a novel pattern of crime (Ndubueze, 2013). With the development of digital technology came the transportation of diverse forms of crimes, deviance and terror into the cyber space.

Cyber infrastructure have triggered a boom in online crime and criminality. The safe haven of some sort that the Internet provides for criminal elements have meant that they will migrate from the physical space to the cyber space. Expectedly, traditional crimes like Advance Fee Fraud, money laundering, kidnapping and now committed using the Internet infrastructure. Gordon (2003 p. 8) observed that "currently almost half of the 30 groups on the State Department's list of terrorist organizations have their own websites, which can be used to solicit money from their various causes or disseminate coded message, either explicitly or steganograhically.

Furthermore, the space transition traffic is ridiculously youngsters-heavy. Recently, Ndubueze (2013, p. 1) have augured that "the internet and particularly the social media has become one of the strongest platforms for young to people express and engage themselves in a virtual world that beats the barriers of highly policed borders." These youth often referred to as the "Generation Y" or the "Millennials" or the "Net Generation" are technology-savvy and Internet-obsessed. They are migrating in their thousands from the real world space to the virtual space, often unguided, unsupervised and worst un-precautionary. The Generation y because of the logic of number, perhaps constitute the weakest link in the transition chain and as such the most vulnerable. These young adults can easily be brainwashed online and recruited by terrorist groups without their parents and guardians knowing. Ultimately, a strongly motivated, ready-army of youngsters who owe unflinching allegiance to a cause they believe in and are willing to pursue with all their breath is created. The internet provides them with a platform to effectively enroll and engage with such terrorist organizations, whiling skillfully managing parental and "significant others" oversights and trails. Thus, on this new platform (the internet) terrorist affiliation, indoctrination and mobilization is relatively easier, swifter, "safer," wider and perhaps guarantees far more Return On Investment (ROI) for the financiers. Thus the internet occupies a strategic position in the terrorism value chain.

## The Perspectives: Tenor of the Discourses on Policing Cyber Terrorism

It has been argued that terrorist, groups from birth will continue to develop and eventually die after reaching the last stage of their campaign (Iqbal & De Silva, 2013), but while they exist, they develop capabilities and capacities for causing wide-scale grievous harm to targets (hard or soft), including those online. Thus, scholars and researchers have begun to show interest in developing paradigms for policing cyber terrorism. But the lack of consensus on the scope of cyberterrorism definition has remained one of the major drawbacks of policing in this emerging problem. Heickero (2014) observes that the academic discussion on cyber terrorism is polarized along two perspectives. First, there are those who contend that the threats are real, substantial, given that vulnerabilities multiply when many different systems integrated, controlled and run through computers. This perspective is held by governments and security firms. Second, here we have those who opine that there is no threat at all or only a small threat. They maintain that there are no or only a few identified cases of cyberterrorism. The belief is that cyberterrorism concern is exaggerated and that this serves the interest of security firms. This perspective is propagated by scientists and analysists at universities and research institutes. It is important to note that the side of this debate on which the key stakeholders stand will have serious implications for cyber security policy and policing initiatives/strategies. This perhaps explains where there is dearth of cyberterrorism-specific scientific research, when compared to scientific researches on classical terrorism.

Gordon and Ford (2003) while acknowledging that combating cyber terrorism and classical terrorism would require the regular practice of deterrence, law, defense, negotiation and diplomacy among others with an expanded scope for the former (i.e., cyber terrorism) , maintain that the real impact of the computer on the terrorism scenario is wider than the commonly shared notion of premediated, politically motivated attack perpetrated against information, computer systems, computer programs, and data by sub-national or clandestine elements.

Marcum (2014) observe that vigilantic and legislative efforts to combat cyberterrorism have increased and that private individuals and groups have on their own sought to infiltrate terrorists' websites and deface or alert relevant authorizes about them. Of concern is how much can people with terrorist tendencies, orientation and attributes be deterred. Liberman (2013) contends that deterrence success has not worked for deterrence practitioners and theorists of the subject for over 60 years, He argues further that after the 9/11 al Qaeda terrorist attack on the United States, it was widely believed that success will be difficult to achieve terrorists organizations, rouge states and non-state actors were motivated by religion, irrational and could die for their cause. In the same vein, Stein (as cited in Liberman, 2013) notes that although deterring terrorism may not be unlikely in theory but would in practice because leaders of terrorist organizations may be driven by strong emotional reactions as opposed to the rational cost-benefit calculus of the deterrence theory. These perspectives suggest that policing cyber terrorism is much more complex task than researchers and practitioners have come to appreciate. No policing paradigm or strategy will produce sustainable and measurable result, if it fails to take into due cognizance the inherent complexity of the cyber terrorism problem, the fact that no single model that can produce a quick fix of the problem, the fact that no single government, law enforcement agency or sector can win this war alone and above all the fact that the search for answers to cyber security questions will understandably remain a work in progress.

## The Problem: Understanding the Threat and Vulnerability Landscape

> Cyberterrorism has a short history: Only in the past decade have cyber security threats surfaced worldwide. Obviously targets of cyberterrorism consists of critical infrastructures- including transportation, electronic power grids, oil and gas distribution, telecommunications, air traffic, and financial institutions (Olimstead & Siraj, 2003, p. 16).

In the twenty-first century globalized and digitalized world, critical infrastructures largely drive the social economic, political and military systems of nation states and therefore have huge impact on the lives of both the government and its people. Nonetheless, critical infrastructures are not disruption-proof. Concerns are growing across the globe that terrorist elements are increasingly exploiting the security loop-holes in nations' critical infrastructure to perpetrate terrorist's acts/attacks. There is consensus among scholars and experts that critical infrastructure would constitute one of the major targets of terrorists organization across the world in the post September 11, 2001 attack of the World Trade Centre, United States of America. Wilson (2005) observes that cyber terrorists use their technical expertise to exploit the vulnerabilities in government online security system and critical infrastructure. Moteff, Copeland & Fischer (2003) argue that although critical infrastructure was originally conceived as those whose disruption may cause serve military and economic dislocation, it now includes national monuments, which if attacked may result to massive loss of life and negatively affect the nations morale. Weimann (2005) opines that whereas hackers and terrorists do not share the same inspiration, terrorists may in principle follow the hackers lead to break into government and private computer system in order to shut-down or disrupt the military, financial, and service sectors of developed economies.

It is reported that between 1968 and 2003 there were over 6,100 transnational terrorists' attacks, resulting in over 36,000 deaths and injuries (Mickolvus, Sander, Mudorck & Flemin as cited in Robinson, Crenshaw and Jenkins, 2006). Between 1997 and 2007 there were about 522 terrorist acts, leading to 8,477 injuries, and 2614 fatalities. 73 percent of these incidents were said to be domestic, while 27 percent were transnational (Memorial Institute for the Prevention of Terrorism, as cited in Agbiboa, 2013). According to the 2015 Global Terrorism Index Results terrorist activities increased by 80 per cent in 2014 to an all-time high level. Death from terrorism rose from 18,111 in 2013 to 32,685 in 2014. The report further reveals that the number of people who as a result of terrorist activities increased nine-fold since the year 2000 and that five countries namely: Iraq, Nigeria, Afghanistan, Pakistan and Syria accounted for 78 per cent of the deaths and fifty-seven per cent of all attacks. It indicates that the economic cost of terrorism increased by 61 per cent in 2014 reaching its highest ever level at US dollar 52.9 billion.

## Prospects: Approaches and Strategies for Policing the Cyber Space

> Lack of effective communication, coordination, collaboration and information sharing among military, civilian government elements, international organizations, nongovernmental organizations, private sector, and affected/host nation elements that form the network of partners and stakeholders involved in complex operations such as humanitarian assistance, disaster relief, security, stability, and reconstruction are consistent factors impacting the ability to conduct more successful operations (Wentz, 2011, p. 83).

There are clearly some policy and information gap in management and control of cyber terrorism within and among nations. Losavvio and Shutt (2011) argue that cyber space policy have not sufficiently encouraged protective behaviors in the cyber community. Earlier, Obi (2008, p. 131) opines that:

The Economic Community of West African States (ECOWAS), the New Partnership for Africa's Development (NEPAD) and the African Union (AU) have demonstrated a lot of initiative in relation to the signing of various protocols based on a holistically regionally coordinated approach towards the prevention and combating of terrorism. However, the political and economic realities characterized by fragile democracies, a crisis of development and an apparent lack of political will by the ruling elite(s), have tended to work against the emergence of an autonomous and people-centred regional security system.

Nagvanshi, Sharma, & Raj (2011) argue that terrorism violates human rights and norms of human dignity and personal security that makes peaceful existence possible in society.

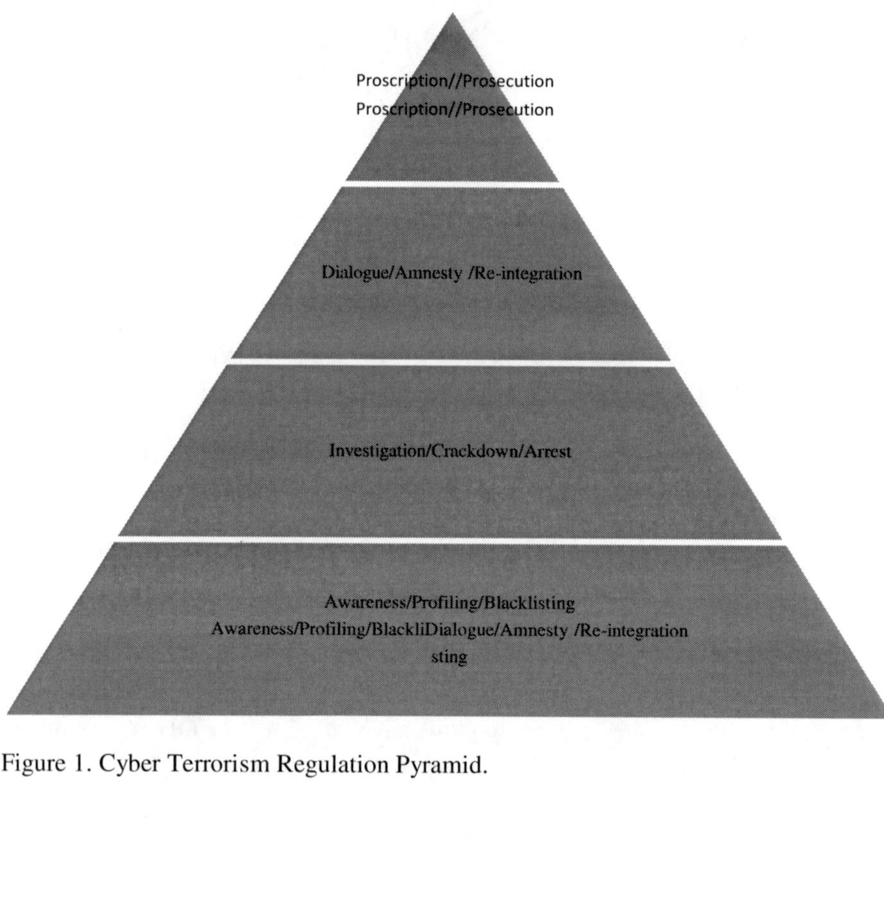


Figure 1. Cyber Terrorism Regulation Pyramid.

## STRATEGIES FOR POLICING CYBER TERRORISM IN AFRICA

### The Regulation Strategy

Terrorist organizations in their life cycle experience a metamorphosis. Sometimes, they start off as a legitimate and registered organizations with overtly noble aims and objectives but with covert terrorist agenda. Conversely, some organizations formed originally to purse lawful ends may drift towards terrorism. Thus, in order to effectively regulate terrorist organizations governments particularly those of Africa may consider adopting a four-level regulatory approach. The will be discussed more extensively below. Although the above regulatory formula is prescribed for policing cyber terrorism, it may also be relevant for the management and control of classical terrorism since the basic elements of both traditional and cyber terrorism are essentially the same. The distinction is obviously in the sphere of influence and perhaps m*odus operandi.*

#### *Awareness, Profiling and Blacklisting*

Intelligence agencies like the State Security Services (SSS) or secret service should increase the tempo of their routine background checks on groups with questionable objectives. This is regardless whether they are ethnic, religious or political, professional or ideological. Given the proliferation of organizations across the world, the criteria for inclusion and exclusion on the intelligence profile list becomes all the more herculean. There are perhaps hundreds of thousands of associations and social groups operating in developing countries of Africa. A data base of such organizations should be periodically updated by the relevant authorities and sent to relevant intelligence/security agencies for necessary profiling. Organizations reasonably suspected to have terrorist agenda, affiliation or sympathy should be flagged and blacklisted.

#### *Investigation, Crackdown, Arrest*

Effort should be made to closely monitor and track the activities of blacklisted organizations. If after thorough investigation, it is found that such organization's activities obviously constitute a potential threat to national security, they should be stopped. The leaders and members of such organizations should be arrested for further investigation. The objective here will be to ascertain who they are (family and friend ties), what exactly they want (aims and objectives), who their financiers (sponsors) are, their involvement in any past terrorist activity locally or international (history), their international link (s) (if any). Also, the investigation should probe if they plan any future attacks and the potential targets of such attacks. This however needs to be done within the ambit of the law and without undue abuse of the fundamental human rights of suspects.

### *Dialogue, Amnesty and Re-Integration*

One of the reasons why terrorists groups emerge is to either redress perceived marginalization suffered by the group or bring it to public knowledge. It is perhaps for this singular reason that terrorist groups like media publicity. Again, this is probably why they would normally claim responsibility for the attacks perpetrated by them. This is where terrorists differ from criminals. While the former courts publicity, the latter abhors it. Dialogue with such groups is an essentially key to solving the problem and appealing to their sentiments. Besides, this dialogue should be friendly as opposed to being adversarial. The group leaders wield huge influence within the terrorist sub-culture and should be invited for talks with the government and those they hold in high esteem like religious leaders etc. should be part of the meeting. The overall objective here will be to find out what exactly they want and then talk terms with them. In the spirit of give and take, a mutually agreed and beneficial position is reached by both parties. Once a consensus is reached at this point, the government grants amnesty to the terrorist group and its members. The concerned government ministry then draw a re-orientation programme for members. This will go a long way in reintegrating them into society's mainstream culture and dilute their terrorist tendencies. Again, this will be done without compromising national sovereignty, national security and national interest.

### *Proscription and Prosecution*

Should the effort at the third level (dialogue, amnesty and re-integration) fail, then the government is left with no other option than to proscribe the organization. Leaders and members of the organization at this point should be apprehended and arranged in court. If found guilty, they should face the punishment prescribed by the extant laws. Care should be taken to ensure that whatever that is done at this level, just like in the previous ones is within the purview of the law of the land as well as in tandem with international best practices.

Overall, it is important to note that as the regulation pyramid goes up, it narrows down, thereby suggesting that there would be a corresponding streamlining taking place at the top of the pyramid. The last two level are critical and of course the "breaking points." Tacit and high degree of expertise and understanding is required by relevant regulatory agencies or statutory committees such as the presidential amnesty committee (established by the out-gone Nigerian president) to go through the whole process of qualifying a group for presidential amnesty or recommending it for proscription and prosecution. Usually, the last level of regulation on the pyramid should only be applied as a last resort, in other words, when all other options below it have failed.

Furthermore, in addition to the regulation pyramid discussed above, the following approaches will be quite useful in securing the cyber space of developing countries from terrorists' activities and potential attacks.

## A Five-Point Integrated Approach for Securing African Cyber Space

### *Conceptual Approach*

Unless African governments, legislators, law enforcement/intelligence agencies and all stake holders are agreed on what constitute and do not constitute terrorism, it may be difficult to effectively tackle it. The tiny dividing line between crime and terrorism need to be clearly defined and agreed upon. All relevant legal frameworks and legislations should as a matter of urgency, be revised to incorporate a broader definition of terrorism that will include the cyber component to it.

### *Benchmarking Approach*

Efforts should be made by all those involved in the policing and regulation of terrorism to understand very deeply how terrorists operate. This way it is easy to benchmark which organization is terrorist and which is not. This is fundamental if the fight against terrorism is to succeed. Branding a group terrorist when the group is not is a flaw that will raise very fundamental issues for the whole exercise of policing and regulation, thus care and rigour is required here. Developing a checklist that will help in qualifying terrorist organization will give boost to the war against terrorism in Africa.

***Policy and Regulation Approach***

The current strategy deployed by regulatory agencies seems to be reactive. There is need to re-engineer Africa's cyber security and regulatory frameworks to make them relevant to emerging threats like cyber terrorism. A special (distinct) national cyber terrorism working group should be established in all African states where they do not already exist. This group will bring together experts and researchers in the academia, ICT sector, intelligence agencies, the police and relevant government ministries to brainstorm on the problem of cyber terrorism and advise the government on appropriate policy in this sphere.

***Socio-Psychological Approach***

Fundamentally, terrorism is a symptom of a more deep-seated social problem and effort to manage and control it must first deal with the critical issue that give rise to terrorism in the first place. The expert knowledge of sociologist, criminologists, psychologists and political scientist would be relevant in understanding what drives terrorist behavior. The objective here is to understand what is on the terrorist's mind, his/her world view and how these combine to influence his/her choices and overt course of action. The governments of Africa should fund researches on this area as wealth of insight into the dynamics of the problem could come from the academia. This may define and shape the policy direction of governments.

***Social Intervention Approach***

Terrorism, insurgency and militancy can be linked to some social problems in society. Social conditions like youth unemployment, poverty, illiteracy and marginalization (be they perceived or real) can fuel these social vices. For instance, an army of unemployed youth will provide a ready "force" for terrorist brainwashing and recruitment. Youth who are gainfully employed may not be incentivized to pursue terrorist's careers. Obviously, terrorist may have a hard time enrolling this category of youth. Furthermore, value re-orientation through radio and television jingles will have huge impact on the world view of young adults and may be the game changer for them. Silke (2003, p. 51) perhaps amplified the essence of this approach in his following thought stimulating words:

> Terrorism is a very old and very persistent problem. It emerges again and again simply because human nature is what it is, and the circumstances that produce it continue to occur across time and

geography. Usually terrorist violence is a symptom of other more fundamental problems. A good appreciation of the psychology of terrorists, though, can open up genuine avenue for lasting peace. One can only hope that events like September 11 will encourage a wider appreciation of the knowledge that we currently have, rather than simply ingrain further the myths and innuendo that have dominated for so long.

## CONCLUSION

Although cases of cyber terrorism in developing countries of Africa have not been fully documented in scientific literature, there are obvious signs that cyber terrorism threats are real and emerging. Of serious concern is the fact that the net effect of any successful cyber terrorist attack in these economies would be very devastating given the growing traffic on the Internet and computer mediated communication super high way. This chapter argued that the transition from the physical space to the cyber space in developing countries is all time high. This transition though a laudable developmental stride is not without some downsides. The downside is an explosion of deviance, crime and terror on the cyber space on a scale that draws all stakeholders to a point of puzzle. The Routine Activity Theory (RAT) was used to orientate the discourse of the perspectives, problems and prospects of cyber terrorism in developing nations of Africa. This chapter calls for an integrated approach in the prevention, management and control of cyber terrorism in developing countries of Africa. To win the war against terrorism in all its forms and dimensions, African governments need to review the sustainability of its current policy and regulatory strategies. It is the contention of this chapter that when terror control measures and initiatives are tilted towards ameliorating the social conditions that give rise to terrorist activities and insurgency like youth unemployment, poverty, illiteracy and marginalization (be they perceived or real), much more sustainable progress will be made in the fight against terrorism.

## REFERENCES

------ (2012a). Cyber Crime and Third Party Policing in Nigeria: A Study of Selected Cybercafes in Lagos Metropolis. An Unpublished Ph.D Thesis. University of Nigeria, Nsukka, Enugu State.

----- (2012b). Regulatory Agencies, Third Parties and Cyber Crime Control in Nigeria. *Bayero Sociologists – A Journal of Sociological Studies,*1, (3.) pp. 116-135.

Adler, F., Muller, G. O. W., & Laufer, W. S. (1998). *Criminology* (3rd ed.). Boston: McGraw Hil.

Agbiboa, D. E. (2013). (Sp)oling domestic terrorism? Boko Haram and state repronse. *Peace Review*, 25: 3, 431 – 438. DOI: 10.1080/10402659. 2013.816571.

Aseniero, G. (1985). A reflection on developmentalism: From development to transformation. In H. Addo. *Development as Social Transformation.* London: Hodder & Stoughton, pp 48-85.

Bachmann, M. (2007). Differential cyber-crime risk awareness and exposure of American internet users: An empirical test of routine activity theory. American Society of Criminology. Retrieved from http://www.all. academic.com/meta/p202126 _index.html.

Briassouls, H. (2001). Sustainable development and its indicators. Through a (Planner's) glass darkly. *Journal of Environmental Planning and Management*, 44 93), 409 – 427.

Chiedozie, I. (2013). Nigeria's critical assets under terrorists' threat, *The Punch*, 17, 26, 481, p. 7.

Ciegis, R. Ramanaukiene, J., & Martinkas, B., (2009). The concept of sustanibale development and its use for sustainability scenarios. *Inzinerine Ekonomiks – Engineering Economics*, 2, pp. 28 – 37.

Clarke, R. V. & Felson, M. (eds.) (1993). *Routine activity and rational choice. Advances in Criminological Theory*, 5. New Brunswick, NJ: Transaction Books.

Cohen, L. E., & Felson, M. (1979). Social change and crime rate trends: A routine activity approach. *American Sociological Review,* 44, 588-608.

Crenshew, M. (1990). Questions to be answered, research to done. In W. Reich (Ed.). *Origi ns of Terrorism*. Cambridge: Woodrow Wileton Center.

Cullen, F. T., Agnew, R. & Wilcox, P. (2014). *Criminological Theory: Past to Present* (5th Ed.). New York: Oxford University Press.

Dempesy, J. S. & Frost, L. S. (2008). *An introduction to policing* (4th Ed.). Belmont, CA. Thompson Higher Education.

Denning, D. (2000). Cyberterrorrism. Testimony before the Special Oversight Panel of Terrorism Committee on Armed Servcies, US House of Representatives, 23 May, 2000. Retrieved March, 16, 2016 from on from http://www.cs.georgetown.edu/-denning/infosec/cyberterror.html.

Eruvbetine, A. (2008). Terrorism: Perplexing Perspectives. In A. Olukoju & M. Falaiye (Eds.). *Global Understanding in the age of Terrorism.* Lagos, Uinversity of Lagos Press. pp. 1-12.

Felson, M. (1998). *Crime and everyday life*, Second Edition. Thousand Oaks, CA: Pine Forge Press.

Felson, M., & Clarke, R. V. (1998). Opportunity makes the thief. *Police Research Series*, Paper 98. Retrieved from skywallnet.com/dataserver/CA/OMT_PP_CP.pdf.

Gibbs, J. P. (1989). Conceptualization of terrorism. *American Sociological Review,* 54 (3), 329 – 340.

Goodwin, J. (2006). A theory of categorical terrorism. *Social Forces.* 84 (4), 2027 – 2046.

Gordon, S. & Ford, R. (2003). Cyberterrorism? Symantac security Reponse. White Paper. Retrieved September 16, 2013 from http://www.symantec.com/avcenter/reference/cyber terrorism.pdf.

Gori, U. (2009). Intriduction. In U. Gori (Ed.). *Modelling cyber security: approaches, models, strategies*. pp. vii-xviii. IOS Press.

Goulet, D. (1995). Autthentic development and its sustainability. In Tryzna (Ed.) *Defining and Measuring Sustainable Development.* California: International Center For Environment and Public Policy, pp. 44 – 59.

Heickerb, R. (2014). Cyber terrorism: Electronic Jihad. *Strategic Analysis*, 38 (4), 554 – 565, DOI: 10.1080/097001612014.918435.

Igbal, K. & De Silum, S. (2013). Terrorists lifestyles: A case of study of Tehrik-e-Taliban Parkistan *Journal of Policing and Counter Terrorism*, 8 (1), 72-86. doi: 10.1020/18335330.2013.789399.

Laqueur, W. (1977). *Terrorism.* London: Weidanfied and Nicolson.

Leukfeldt, R., Veenstra, S., Stool, W. (20130. High volume cybetr crime and the organization of the police: The results of two empirical studies in the Netherlands. *International Journal of Cyber Criminology,* 7 (1), 1-17.

Lieberman, E. (2013). Dettering terrorism: Elusive, marginal, or strtageic? Contemporary Security Policy, 34, (1). 223 – 232. doi: 10.1080/1352 3260.2013.771066.

Losavio, M., & Shutt, J. E. (2011). The information polity: Social and legal frameworks for critical cyber infrastructure protection. In T. Saadawi & L. Jordan (Eds.) *Cyber infrastructure protection.* Carlisle, PA: Strategic Studies Institute, U.S. Army War College, pp. 129- 158.

Marcum, C. D. (2014). *Cyber Crime.* New York: Wolters Kluwer law & Business.

Moteff, J., Copeland, C. & Fischer, J. (2003). Critical infrastructure: What makes an infrastructure critical? Report for Congress. Available at: http://www.fas.org/irp/crs/RL31556.pdf.

Nagvanshi, J, Sharma, A. & Raj, M. (2011). Human rights, terrorism and security laws in India. In K. Jaishankar and N. Ronel (Eds.) *Proceedings of the First International Conference of the South Asian Society of Criminology and Victimology (SASCV).* Tirunelveli, India: SASCV & Department of Criminology and Criminal Justice, Manommarriam Sundaranar University. pp. 17 - 19.

Ndubueze, P. N. & Igbo E. U. M. (2014). Third Parties and Cyber Crime Policing in Nigeria: Some Reflections. *Policing: A Journal of Policy and Practice.* 8 (1): 59 – 68.

Ndubueze, P. N. (2013). Generation Y and Online Victimization in Nigeria: How vulnerable are younger respondents? A paper delivered at the Second international Conference of the South Asian Society of Criminology and Victimology (SASCV) January 11-13, 2013 at Kanyakumari, Tamil Nadu, India.

Nicaso, A. & Lamothe, L. (2005). *Angels, Mobsters & Narco-Theorists: the Rising menace of global criminal empires.* Ontario: John Wiley & Sons Canada.

Obi, C. (2008). West African security in the context of the global war on terror: Some reflections. In A. Olukoju & M. Falaiye. (Eds.). *Global Understanding in the age of Terrorism.* Lagos, University of Lagos Press. Pp 111-136.

Olmstead, S. & Siraj, A. (2009). Cyberterrorism: The threat of virtual warfare. CrossTalk: The *Journal of Defense Software Engineering*, November/December.

Onapaju, H., Uzodike, U. O. & whetho, A. (2012). Boko Haram terrorism in Nigeria: The International Dimension. *South African Journal of International Affairs*, 19, (3), 337 – 357. doi: 10.1080/10220461. 2012.740319.

Robison, K. K.; Crenshaw, E. M. & Jenkins, J. C. (2006). Ideologies of violence. The social origins of Islamist and leftist transnational terrorism. *Social Froces,* 64 (4), 2009 – 2026.

Rogers, M. (2003). The Psychology of cyber terrrorismt. In A. Silke (Ed.). *Terrorists, Victims and Society: Psychological Perspectives on Terrorism and Its Consequences* (pp. 77-92). England: John Wiley & Sons.

Roscini, M. (2014). Cyber operatives as Nuclear counterproliferation measures. *Journal of Conflict & Security Law*. 19 (1), 133 – 157. doi: 10.109/jcsl/krt028.

Silke, A. (2003). Becoming a terrorist. In A. Silke (Ed.). *Terrorists, Victims and Society: Psychological Perspectives on Terrorism and Its Consequences*. England: john Wiley & Sons.

The Terrrorism (Prevention) Act, 2011.The 2015 Global Terrorism Index Results. Retrieved March 15, 2015 from http://economicsandpeace.org/wp-content/uploads/2015/11/Global-Terrorism-Index-2015.pdf.

UN Economic Commission for Europe 92009). Measuring sustainable development. Newyork: United Nations.

United Nations Economic Commission for Africa (2013). Mankin the most of Africa's commodities: Industrializing for growth, jobs and economic transformation. Economic Report.

United Nations Economic Commission for Africa (2014). Tackling the challanegs of cybersecurity in Africa. Policy Brief. Retrrieved March 15, 2016 from, http://www.uneca.org/sites/default/files/PublicationFiles/ntis_policy_brief_1.pdf.

US Army TRADOC (2008). Kiddnapping and terror in the contemporary operational environment. Handbook N0. 106. Retrieved September 16, 2013 from http://d esint_threats.heaven.worth.army.mil.

Waugh, W.L. (2001). Managing terrorism as an environmental hazard, In A. Farazamand (Ed.), *Handbook of Crisis Energy Management* (pp. 659-76). New York: M. Dekker, Inc.

Weimann, G. (2005). Cyberterrism: The sum of all fears. *Studies in Conflict and Terrosim*. 28: 129 – 149.

Wentz, L. (2011). The role of cyber power in humanitarian assistance/disaster relief (HA/DR) and stability and reconstruction operations. In T.Saadawi & L. Jordan (Eds.) *Cyber infrastructure protection*. Carlisle, PA: Strategic Studies Institute, U.S. Army War College, pp. 81 -125.

Wilson, C. (2005). Computer *attack and cyber terrorism: Vulnerabilities and policy issues for congress.* Retrieved on September 15, 2013 from http//www.histroy.navy.mil/library/online/comupterattack.htm.

Worrall, J. L. & Schmalleger, F. (2016). *Policing* ($2^{nd}$ Ed.). Poston: Pearson.

## About the Author

**Name: PHILIP N. NDUBUEZE, PhD**
Department of Sociology
Federal University Dutse, Jigawa State, Nigeria
E-mail: philipndubueze@yahoo.com

Philip N. Ndubueze holds a PhD in Criminology and Criminal Justice from the University of Nigeria, Nsukka, Nigeria. He is a lecturer in the Department of Sociology, Federal University Dutse, Jigawa State, Nigeria. He has published several articles in referred local and international journals. His research interests include: cyber criminology, crime prevention/control strategies, penology, victimology and third party policing.

# BIBLIOGRAPHY

*21st Century Policing: Final Report of the Presidential Task Force and Views on the Future of Community Policing* LCCN: 2015510371 Main title: 21st Century Policing: Final Report of the Presidential Task Force and Views on the Future of Community Policing Published/Created: [S.l.]: Nova Science, 2016. Description: p. cm. ISBN: 1634841026 9781634841023

*A sense of justice: legal knowledge and lived experience in Latin America* LCCN: 2015034973 Main title: A sense of justice: legal knowledge and lived experience in Latin America/edited by Sandra Brunnegger and Karen Ann Faulk. Published/Produced: Stanford, California: Stanford University Press, 2016. Description: pages cm ISBN: 9780804797962 (cloth: alk. paper) 9780804799072 (pbk: alk. paper) LC classification: KH99.S46 2016 Authors: Brunnegger, Sandra, 1976- editor. Faulk, Karen Ann, 1976- editor. Contents: Introduction: making sense of justice/Karen Ann Faulk and Sandra Brunnegger -- Transitional justice, memory, and the emergence of legal subjectivities in Colombia/Juan Pablo Vera Lugo -- Pursuing justice in Jewish Buenos Aires/Karen Ann Faulk -- Justice, rights, and discretionary space in Brazilian policing/Graham Denyer Willis -- Imaginaries of judicial practice among legal experts in Argentina/Leticia Barrera -- The craft of justice-making through the permanent peoples' tribunal in Colombia/Sandra Brunnegger -- On justice, insecurity, and the right to the city in Brazil's oldest metropolis/Marta Magalhães Wallace -- Water justice, mining, and the fetish form of law in the Atacama Desert/Alonso Barros -- Conclusion: justice at the limits of law/Mark Goodale. Subjects: Law--Social aspects--South America. Justice--Social aspects--South America. Notes: Includes bibliographical references and index.

*Accountability in policing LCCN: 2015007788 Main title: Accountability in policing*/edited by Stuart Lister and Michael Rowe. Published/Produced: Abingdon, Oxon; New York, NY: Routledge, 2016. Description: xv, 237 pages; 24 cm. ISBN: 9780415715331 (hardback) LC classification: HV7935 .A25 2016 Authors: Lister, Stuart. Rowe, Michael, 1967- Subjects: Police administration. Police. Responsibility. Series: Routledge frontiers of criminal justice; 29

*Aid under fire: nation building and the Vietnam War* LCCN: 2016011182 Author/Editor: Elkind, Jessica Breiteneicher, 1976- author. Main title: Aid under fire: nation building and the Vietnam War/Jessica Elkind. Published/Produced: Lexington, Kentucky: University Press of Kentucky, [2016] Description: pages cm ISBN: 9780813165837 (hardcover: alk. paper) LC classification: DS556.9 .E55 2016 Summary: "In the aftermath of World War II, as longstanding empires collapsed and former colonies struggled for independence, the US employed new diplomatic tools to counter challenges to its interests across the globe. Among the most important new strategies was development assistance-the attempt to strengthen alliances by providing technology, financial aid, and administrators to fledgling states in order to disseminate and inculcate American practices in local populations. While the US implemented development programs in several nations, nowhere were these policies more significant than in Vietnam. In Aid Under Fire, Jessica Elkind examines US nation-building efforts in the South Vietnamese state during the decade before the ground war. Based on archival sources and interviews with aid workers, this study demonstrates how the official US aid agency as well as several nongovernmental organizations implemented nearly every component of nonmilitary assistance given to South Vietnam, including public and police administration, agricultural development, education, and public health. Despite the sincerity of American efforts, most Vietnamese citizens understood them to be little more than a continuation of attempts by foreign powers to dominate their homeland. Elkind argues that, instead of reexamining their core assumptions or their approach as violence in the region escalated, US policymakers and aid workers only strengthened their commitment to nation building, increasingly modifying their goals to support counterinsurgency efforts. Aid Under Fire highlights the important role played by nonstate actors in advancing US policies and reveals in stark terms the limits of American power and influence during the period widely considered to be the apex of US supremacy in the world."--Provided by publisher. Contents: Introduction: building South Vietnam -- "The Virgin Mary is going south": refugee resettlement in South Vietnam -- Civil servants and cold warriors: technical assistance in public administration -- Sowing the seeds of discontent: American agricultural-development programs in South Vietnam -- Policing the insurgency: police administration and internal security in South Vietnam -- Teaching loyalty: Educational development and the strategic hamlet program -- Conclusion: "Ears of stone." Subjects: United States. Operations Mission to Vietnam. Nation-building--Vietnam (Republic) Technical assistance, American--Vietnam (Republic) Intercultural communication--Vietnam (Republic)--Case studies. Military assistance, American--Vietnam (Republic) Economic assistance, American--Vietnam (Republic) Vietnam (Republic)--Politics and government. Vietnam (Republic)--Economic conditions. United States--Foreign relations--Vietnam (Republic) Vietnam (Republic)--Foreign relations--United States. Notes: Includes bibliographical references and index. Series: Studies in conflict, diplomacy and peace

*Chasing ghosts: the policing of terrorism* LCCN: 2015031238 Author/Editor: Mueller, John E., author. Main title: Chasing ghosts: the policing of terrorism/John Mueller, Mark G. Stewart. Published/Produced: Oxford; New York: Oxford University Press, [2016] Description: viii, 391 pages; 25 cm ISBN: 9780190237318 (hardcover) LC classification: HV6432 .M837 2016 Authors: Stewart, Mark G., 1961- author. Subjects: Terrorism--Prevention--United States. Terrorism--Prevention--United States--Costs. National security--United States--Costs. Intelligence service--United States. Police--United States. Civil rights--United States. Notes: Includes bibliographical references (pages 375-376) and index.

*Collaborative policing: police, academics, professionals, and communities working together for education, training, and program implementation* LCCN: 2016285025 Main title: Collaborative policing: police, academics, professionals, and communities working together for education, training, and program implementation/edited by Peter C. Kratcoski, Maximilian Edelbacher. Published/Produced: Boca Raton, Fla.: CRC Press, [2016]. Description: xxxix, 316 pages: illustrations; 25 cm. ISBN: 9781482251401 148225140X LC classification: HV8142 C62 2016 Authors: Edelbacher, Max, editor. Kratcoski, Peter C., 1936- editor. Contents: Section 1. Police and academic collaboration in research, education, and training -- section 2. Collaboration among the police, professional practitioners, and the community in the criminal justice process and in crime prevention programs.

Subjects: Police--Study and teaching. Police training. Academic-industrial collaboration. Notes: Includes bibliographical references and index Series: Advances in police theory and practice series Advances in police theory and practice series.

*Comparative, international and global justice: perspectives from criminology and criminal justice* LCCN: 2015020344 Author/Editor: Banks, Cyndi, author. Main title: Comparative, international and global justice: perspectives from criminology and criminal justice/Cynthia L. Banks, James Baker. Published/Produced: Los Angeles, California: Sage Publications, 2016. Description: xvii, 571 pages; 26 cm ISBN: 9781483332383 (pbk.: alk. paper) LC classification: K5001 .B36 2016 Authors: Baker, James, 1948- author. Contents: Introduction -- Comparative criminal justice: comparing crime across countries -- Systems of law: common law, civil law, socialist law, Islamic law, indigenous law -- Policing -- Courts and criminal procedure -- Punishment -- Juvenile justice -- Transitional justice: justice, forgiveness and impunity -- The International Criminal Court -- Transnational crime -- Human trafficking across borders -- Terrorism -- Violence against women -- Human rights and cultural relativism: female circumcision and child soldiers. Subjects: Criminal justice, Administration of. Comparative law. International criminal law. International law and human rights. Criminology. Notes: Includes bibliographical references (pages 495-527) and index.

*Contentious politics in Africa: identity, conflict, and social change* LCCN: 2016002651 Meeting name: Africa Conference (Tex.) (2013: University of Texas at Austin) Main title: Contentious politics in Africa: identity, conflict, and social change/edited by Toyin Falola and Wanjala S. Nasong'o. Published/Produced: Durham, North Carolina: Carolina Academic Press, 2016. Description: pages cm ISBN: 9781611637427 (alk. paper) LC classification: JQ1875 .A7236 2013 Authors: Falola, Toyin, editor. Nasong'o, Shadrack Wanjala, editor. Contents: Contentious politics and political change in Africa: introduction/Toyin Falola & Wanjala S. Nasong'o -- Violence, war, and political change -- The Hobbesian concept of self-defense and violence in twenty-first century Africa: a critique/Oladele Abiodun Balogun & Moyosore Balogun -- The war that time forgot: a historiographical examination of the concentration camps of the Second South African War/Kevin Karaki -- Objectivity, ethics, and the Nigerian media in conflict reportage: the case for peace and development journalism/Rofiah Olateju Animashaun -- Chronicling the Nigerian Civil War: a lexico-semantic analysis of Wole Soyinka's Season of anomy and Chimamanda Adichie's Half of a yellow sun/Juliet Nkane Ekpang -- Socioeconomic change and development -- Socio-economic and structural-political change and continuity: post-liberation South Africa, Zimbabwe, and Mozambique/Alexius Amtaika -- Women's movements and political transformation in Kenya: a historical survey/Martha Musalia & Joseph Wasonga -- The politics of evangelization through education and development: Marianist projects in Kenya/C'line A. Jacquemin -- Emotions, displacement, and the new Kenyan/Besi Brillian Muhonja & Gillianne Obaso -- NGO-government interactions in South Africa: possibilities of cross-sector cooperation/Vernon Damani Johnson & Kirsten Lorgen-Knapp -- The role of the southern African development community in the political and economic crisis in Zimbabwe/Kudzai Goto & Malimela Langelihle -- Social movements and identity politics -- Some epistemic, taxonomic, and methodological issues in the consideration of social movements: Niger Delta militancy and "Boko Haram" in Nigeria/P. Okechukwu Eke -- The tyranny of ethno-religious identities and expressions and the survival of the Nigerian state in the twenty-first century/Mike O. Odey -- Globalization and socio-cultural transformations in Nigeria: emerging trends, challenges, and prospects/Israel Dantata Sule -- Fragmented stability: neoliberalism and the politics of belonging in anglophone Cameroon/Nicholas A. Jackson -- The indigene/settler dichotomy and Nigeria's quest for nationhood/Ntim Gyakari Esew -- Politics of revolts and protests -- Youth revolts in apartheid South Africa and contemporary Tunisia: an appraisal/Ntim Gyakari Esew & Agbo Uchechukwu Johnson -- Expressions of dissent and protests: post-election reactions in Nigeria and the future conduct of peaceful elections/Babatunde A. Ojedokun -- Governmentalities of policing protests in military and democratic dispensations in Nigeria: a comparative analysis of June 12, 1993, and January 2012/Gbemisola Abdul-Jelil Animasawun & Yinka Ahmed Aluko. Subjects: Political violence--Africa--Congresses. Africa--Politics and government--1960---Congresses. Africa--Social conditions--1960---Congresses. Africa--Economic conditions--1960---Congresses. Notes: Papers from the 2013 Africa Conference at the University of Texas at Austin. Includes bibliographical references and index. Series: African world series Carolina Academic Press African world series.

*Coping and suicide amongst the lads: expectations of masculinity in post-traditional Ireland* LCCN: 2015028211 Author/Editor: Garcia, Felicia, author. Main title: Coping and suicide amongst the lads: expectations of masculinity in post-traditional Ireland/Felicia Garcia. Published/Produced: New York, NY:

Palgrave Macmillan, 2016. Description: pages cm. ISBN: 9781137530325 (hardback) LC classification: HV6548.I73 G37 2016 Summary: "For every female suicide in Ireland, there are five male suicides. Coping and Suicide amongst the Lads is based on fieldwork in this book was done in and around Cork, Ireland between 2008 and 2012 among some forty young lads, aged 18-34. This anthropological approach aims to help explain why some groups in a specific society or community are more prone to commit suicide than others. In addition to suicide, this book focuses extensively on related issues such as alcohol, drug abuse, and other self-destructive behaviors prominent within Irish lad culture. This includes peer pressures and loyalties, chauvinistic jargon, homophobic bullying, humor, and the culture of mocking so as to grasp the cultural expectations of this particular form of masculinity. The everyday workings of gender segregation and gender-appropriateness is examined in detail by informants while addressing the underlying question whether increased gender equality--which includes men--could lessen young men's vulnerability to self-destructive behaviors and suicide in Ireland"--Provided by publisher. "This in-depth ethnographic account of male suicide in Ireland deals examines the young Irish working class males who are dealing and coping with life's many stressors in ways that differ significantly from their female peers. Irish suicide statistics and local testimonies indicate how gender specific pain and distress really is and what it means to be male in Ireland today"-- Provided by publisher. Contents: Machine generated contents note: -- 1. Introduction2. Theorizing Social Change in Ireland3. Low Income Youth: Autonomy and Independence4. Neo-Traditional Masculinity and Social Change5. Policing and Schooling Gender Appropriate Behavior 6. Consuming the Craic, Destroying the Body 7. Concluding Discussion. Subjects: Suicide--Ireland. Young men--Suicidal behavior--Ireland. Young men--Ireland--Social conditions. Working class men--Ireland--Social conditions. Masculinity--Ireland. Social Science/Anthropology/Cultural. Social Science/Customs & Traditions. Social Science/Men's Studies. Social Science/Death & Dying. Notes: Includes bibliographical references and index. Series: Global masculinities

*Court- martial: how military justice has shaped America from the revolution to 9/11 and beyond* LCCN: 2016002824 Author/Editor: Bray, Chris (Historian), author. Main title: Court- martial: how military justice has shaped America from the revolution to 9/11 and beyond/Chris Bray. Edition: First edition. Published/Produced: New York: W.W.Norton & Company, 2016. Description: pages cm ISBN: 9780393243406 (hardcover) LC classification:

KF7625 .B73 2016 Contents: "Almost a blasphemer": citizen-soldiers as neighbors in the early United States -- "A blind lottery": discipline and justice in the old navy -- "A lawful going home": conflict and coercion in the Jacksonian military -- "I won't be quiet": force and consent in the Civil War -- "Amenable to military law": policing civilians with military authority -- "All that savored of the overseer": black soldiers in the nineteenth century -- "Maniacs or wild beasts": military justice and American expansion -- "We return fighting": black soldiers in the Jim Crow era -- "An emergency condition": World War I and the first debate over reform -- "We've got to live with this the rest of our lives": the deadly justice of World War II -- "You cannot maintain discipline by administering justice": the Cold War and the UCNJ -- "My god, he's firing into the ditch": Vietnam, the hollow army, and the end of the cold war -- Epilogue: the living past: the court-martial in contemporary America. Subjects: Courts-martial and courts of inquiry--United States--History. Notes: Includes bibliographical references and index.

*Covert investigation* LCCN: 2016931036 Author/Editor: Harfield, Clive., author. Main title: Covert investigation/Clive Harfield, MSc, LLM, MA, MPhil, PhD and Karen Harfield, BSc (Hons); with a foreword by Professor John Grieve, CBE, QPM. Edition: Fourth edition. Published/Produced: Oxford, United Kingdom; New York, NY: Oxford University Press, 2016. Description: xxxvii, 265 pages: illustrations; 24 cm. ISBN: 9780198743293 LC classification: KD8335 .H37 2016 Authors: Harfield, Karen. Contents: Navigating a moral minefield -- Statutory principles in covert investigation -- Authorization and governance -- Understanding the operating environment -- Managing covert investigation -- Directed surveillance --- Intrusive surveillance -- Interference with property or wireless telegraphy and entry onto land -- Covert investigation and computers -- Examining mobile phones -- Commmunications data -- Interception of communications -- Covert human intelligence sources -- Covert investigation abroad -- What does good covert investigation look like? Subjects: Undercover operations--Law and legislation--Great Britain. Police patrol--Great Britain--Surveillance operations. Notes: Includes bibliographical references and index. Series: Blackstone's practical policing

*Crime and violence prevention: moving beyond hot-stove policing and perpetrator rehabilitation* LCCN: 2015032802 Main title: Crime and violence prevention: moving beyond hot-stove policing and perpetrator rehabilitation/Myra F. Taylor, Umneea Khan, and Julie Ann Pooley, editors.

Published/Produced: Hauppauge, New York: Nova Science Publishers, Inc., 2016. Description: 357 pages: 26cm. ISBN: 9781634837927 (hardcover) LC classification: HV6025 .C71335 2016 Authors: Taylor, Myra, 1962- editor. Contents: Preface -- Introduction -- Crime and violence prevention: steps towards building a less violent and less crime ridden future society/Myra F. Taylor, Edith Cowan University, Australia -- Public manifestations of violent crime -- Violent assaults: apprehended suspects' mitigating "i'm not sure what happened i was intoxicated" response when questioned by police about a glassing, one-punch hit, or an armed/aggravated robbery incident/Myra F. Taylor, Edith Cowan University, Australia -- Enhancing understanding of glassing assault violence through an analysis of social media responders' apportionment of societal blame/Myra F. Taylor, Georgia Carragher, Edith Cowan University, Australia -- Neighbourhood violence: an initial evaluation of gatecrashers who swarm residential areas and through their unruly actions cause parties to go out-of-control and necessitate police attendance/Myra F. Taylor and Umneea Khan, Edith Cowan University, Australia, and others -- Parental experiences of societal blame -- Mother blame: the resilience and decision-making abilities of mothers with a school-aged child who has been accused of bullying/Erin Jarvis and Myra F. Taylor, Edith Cowan University, Australia -- The influence of parent blame on the willingness of parents of adolescent offenders to participate in court directed parenting programs: a systematic review/Rebecca Eaton and Myra F. Taylor, Edith Cowan University, Australia -- Adolescent involvement in graffiti crime: parents experiences and perspectives on how they and society can work in tandem to deter future offending/Myra F. Taylor, Edith Cowan University, Australia -- There's no support, it's a nightmare trip, but you cope and you get through it: custodial grandparents¿ experiences of raising the child/ren of their incarcerated son/daughter/Myra F. Taylor, Ruth Marquis, Rachel Batten and David Coall, Edith Cowan University, Australia -- Crime and violence prevention initiatives -- Adolescent-to-parent violence: a review of professional responses, the efficacy of these responses, and how they are viewed by parent-victims/Rikki Maynard, David Ryder, and Myra F. Taylor, Edith Cowan University, Australia -- Childhood onset conduct disorder: breaking the cycle of crime and violence early though the implementation of the koolkids school-based interactive intervention program/Stephen Houghton, Annemaree Carroll, Emma Saunders O'Connor, and Jedda Crow, The University of Western Australia, Australia, and others -- A contemporary review of childhood antisocial behaviour in school settings/Emma Saunders O'Connor, Annemaree Carroll, Stephen Houghton, and Caroline Donovan, The

University of Queensland, Australia, and others -- Developing a comprehensive, evidence-based strategy for violence prevention: lessons learned from alberta, canada/Claire Crooks, Lana Wells, and Elizabeth Dozois, Word on the Street Ltd., Canada, and others -- I believe in the hot stove principle of crime prevention policing:educating kids if you do the crime you will get burnt: australian police intelligence officers¿ perspectives on juvenile crime/Myra F. Taylor, Edith Cowan University, Australia -- Prevention of youth gang-related violence: a narrative review/Damien Williams and Claire Williams, University of St Andrews, Fife Scotland, and others -- Desistence from criminal activity and gang membership: evaluating the effectiveness of the voices4peru? sponsored initiative club deportivo dan/Michael Antonio, Susan Shutt, and Christopher Przemieniecki, West Chester University, Pennsylvania, USA, and others -- The effectiveness of life-skills training in violence prevention: a case study in mexico/Susan Pick, Martha Givaudan, and Anna-Emilia Hietanen, National Autonomous University of Mexico, Mexico -- The case for alcohol outlet density controls as a promising approach to prevent domestic violence/Lana Wells, Elena Esina, and Alina Turner, University of Calgary, Alberta, Canada -- Is the youthful repurposed occupation of an abandoned swimming pool an act of prosocial sustainability that could be tolerated, or is it a criminal act that needs to be punished?/Rowena Scott and Myra F. Taylor, Curtin University, Western Australia, and others -- Concluding thoughts -- Changing acceptance of the inevitability of crime and violence: an offender-by-offender, family-by-family, community-by-community, and society-by-society strengthening approach/Myra F. Taylor, Edith Cowan University, Australia -- Acknowledgements and index -- Editors and contributors -- Index. Subjects: Crime. Crime prevention. Violence--Prevention. Notes: Includes index. Series: Law, crime and law enforcement

*Crime, policing and punishment in England,* 1660-1914 LCCN: 2015017471 Author/Editor: Gray, Drew D. Main title: Crime, policing and punishment in England, 1660-1914/Drew D. Gray. Published/Produced: New York: Bloomsbury Academic, 2016. Description: pages cm ISBN: 9781441135636 (hb) 9781441117656 (pb) LC classification: HV9960.G72 G73 2016 Contents: Acknowledgements -- Key themes in the history of crime -- Introduction: methods, themes and debates in the history of crime -- Media and crime -- Violence: the decline of homicide and a growing intolerance towards assault -- The nature of property crime -- The causes of property crime -- Gender & crime in the criminal justice system: women as victims --

Gender & crime: women as perpetrators of crime -- Juvenile crime: from artful dodger to reformatory boy -- The evolution & development of the English criminal justice system -- From parlour to police court: the role of the JP and the emergence of the modern magistrate -- Dogberry to detectives: policing from amateurs to professionals -- Removing the victim?: the changing nature of prosecution in the courts in England -- The decline and fall of the "bloody code": the changing nature of punishment policy in the long eighteenth century -- The rise and fall of incarceration -- Conclusions and suggestions for future research -- Bibliography -- Index. Subjects: Criminal justice, Administration of--England--History. Crime--England--History. Police--England--History. Notes: Includes bibliographical references and index.

*Criminal justice: a brief introduction* LCCN: 2014020181 Author/Editor: Schmalleger, Frank. Main title: Criminal justice: a brief introduction/Frank Schmalleger, Ph.D., Distinguished Professor Emeritus, The University of North Carolina at Pembroke. Edition: Eleventh edition. Published/Produced: Boston: Pearson, [2016] Description: xxiii, 424 [71] pages; 28 cm ISBN: 9780133591316 013359131X LC classification: HV9950 .S34 2016 Contents: What is criminal justice? -- The crime picture -- Criminal law -- Policing: purpose and organization -- Policing: legal aspects -- Policing: issues and challenges -- The courts -- The courtroom work group and the criminal trial -- Sentencing -- Probation, parole, and community corrections -- Prisons and jails -- Prison life -- Juvenile justice. Subjects: Criminal justice, Administration of--United States. Crime--United States. Law enforcement--United States.

*Criminal justice: the essentials* LCCN: 2015014212 Author/Editor: Lab, Steven P. Main title: Criminal justice: the essentials/Steven P. Lab, Bowling Green State University, Marian R. Williams, Appalachian State University, Jefferson E. Holcomb, Appalachian State University, Melissa W. Burek, Bowling Green State University, William R. King Sam Houston State University, Michael E. Buerger, Bowling Green State University. Edition: Fourth Edition. Published/Produced: New York: Oxford University Press, 2016. Description: pages cm ISBN: 9780190272524 LC classification: HV9950 .L33 2015 Authors: Williams, Marian Rebecca. Contents: Crime, criminal justice, and policy -- Issues of law -- Policing and law enforcement -- The court system -- Institutional corrections -- Community corrections -- The juvenile justice system -- Conclusion -- Glossary -- Bibliography -- Index. Subjects: Criminal justice, Administration of--United States. Notes: Revised edition of the authors' Criminal justice, 2013. Includes bibliographical references and index.

*Discursive constructions of consent in the legal process* LCCN: 2015021046 Main title: Discursive constructions of consent in the legal process/edited by Susan Ehrlich, Diana Eades, and Janet Ainsworth. Published/Produced: Oxford, UK; New York, NY: Oxford University Press, [2016] Description: xii, 326 pages; 25 cm. ISBN: 9780199945351 (hardcover: alk. paper) LC classification: K579.I6 .D57 2016 Authors: Ehrlich, Susan (Susan Lynn), editor. Eades, Diana, 1953- editor. Ainsworth, Janet, editor. Contents: Introduction: linguistic and discursive dimensions of consent/Susan Ehrlich and Diana Eades -- Culture, cursing, and coercion: the impact of police officer swearing on the voluntariness of consent to search in police-citizen interactions/Janet Ainsworth -- Post-penetration rape: coercion or freely-given consent?/Susan Ehrlich -- Erasing context in the courtroom construal of consent/Diana Eades -- Talking the ethical turn: drawing on tick-box consent in policing/Frances Rock -- Transparent and opaque consent in contract formation/Lawrence Solan -- The empty performative? Informed consent to genetic research/John Conley, R. Jean Cadigan and Arlene Davis -- Promoting litigant consent to arbitration in multilingual small claims court/Philipp Sebastian Angermeyer -- Consent and compliance in youth justice conferences/Michele Zappavigna, Paul Dwyer and J. R. Martin -- Non-consent and discursive resistance: radical reformulation in a post-sting police interview/Philip Gaines -- Totality of circumstances and translating the Miranda warnings/Susan Berk-Seligson -- Negotiating the right to remain silent in inquisitorial trials/Fleur van der Houwen and Guusje Jol -- "No comment" responses to questions in police investigative interviews/Elizabeth Stokoe, Derek Edwards and Helen Edwards. Subjects: Consent (Law)--Language. English language--Discourse analysis. Notes: Includes bibliographical references and indexes. Series: Oxford studies in language and law

*DIY Detroit: making do in a city without services* LCCN: 2015008728 Author/Editor: Kinder, Kimberley. Main title: DIY Detroit: making do in a city without services/Kimberley Kinder. Published/Produced: Minneapolis: University of Minnesota Press, [2016] Description: pages cm ISBN: 9780816697076 (hc: alk. paper) 9780816697090 (pb: alk. paper) LC classification: HN80.D6 K56 2016 Contents: Introduction: self-provisioning in Detroit -- Do-it-yourself cities -- Seeking new neighbors -- Protecting vacant homes -- Repurposing abandonment -- Domesticating public works -- Policing home spaces -- Producing local knowledge -- Conclusion: triumphs of hope over reason. Subjects: Community development--Michigan--Detroit. Urban renewal--Michigan--Detroit--Citizen participation. Municipal services--Michigan--Detroit--Citizen participation. Civic improvement--Michigan--Detroit. Urban policy--Michigan--Detroit--Citizen participation. Detroit (Mich.)--Economic conditions--21st century. Notes: Includes bibliographical references and index.

*Down, out, and under arrest: policing and everyday life in skid row* LCCN: 2015046039 Author/Editor: Stuart, Forrest, author. Main title: Down, out, and under arrest: policing and everyday life in skid row/Forrest Stuart. Published/Produced: Chicago; London: The University of Chicago Press, 2016. Description: pages cm ISBN: 9780226370811 (cloth: alk. paper) LC classification: HV7936.P8 S78 2016 Contents: Fixing the poor -- The rise of therapeutic policing -- From rabble management to recovery management -- Becoming copwise -- Training for survival -- Cooling off the block -- Policing the police. Subjects: Police-community relations--United States. Urban poor--United States. Notes: Includes bibliographical references and index.

*Environmental crime in transnational context: global issues in green enforcement and criminology* LCCN: 2015034248 Main title: Environmental crime in transnational context: global issues in green enforcement and criminology/by Toine Spapens, Rob White, Wim Huisman. Published/Produced: Farnham, Surrey, UK England; Burlington, VT, USA: Ashgate, 2016. Description: pages cm. ISBN: 9781472469625 (hardback: alk. paper) LC classification: HV6401 .E587 2016 Authors: Spapens, A. C., editor. White, R. D. (Robert Douglas), 1956- editor. Huisman, W. (Wim), editor. Contents: Introduction/Toine Spapens, Rob White and Wim Huisman -- The contested planet: global green criminology, environmental crime and the world/Nigel South -- Tackling cross-border environmental crime: a “wicked problem”/Toine Spapens and Wim Huisman -- Illegal wildlife trade to the EU and harms to the world/Daan van Uhm -- Is green criminology paradigm-breaking?: some reflections on hydrocarbon and resource extraction, crime and criminological thinking/James Sheptycki -- Addressing transnational environmental crime: the role of intelligence-led policing/Carole Gibbs -- Regulatory responses to transnational environmental crime: an overview of choices, challenges and culture/Grant Pink -- Transboundary international fisheries crime and restitution for South Africa: the case of United States v

Bengis, 2013/Jan Glazewski -- Four problems for specialist courts in dealing with nonhuman environmental victims/Rob White -- New environmental governance: environmental harms, enforcement and collaboration/Cameron Holley -- Deliberative democracy and environmental law enforcement/ Giuseppe Rotolo -- Deterring corporate environmental crime: lessons from the waste industry in the Netherlands/Karin van Wingerde -- Enforcing the European emissions trading system within the EU member states: a procrustean bed?/Floor Fleurke and Jonathan Verschuuren -- Criminal networks and black markets in transnational environmental crime/Lorraine Elliott -- Eliciting narratives on the experiences of environmental victimization: a qualitative visual method/Lorenzo Natali -- Organized crime and illegal waste disposal in campania/Pasquale Peluso -- Putting our own animals first!: on the criminalization of the migration of other than human animals/Janine Janssen. Subjects: Offenses against the environment. Offenses against the environment--Law and legislation. Notes: Includes bibliographical references and index. Series: Green criminology

*Eu justice and home affairs law:: (for vol. 1) eu immigration and asylum law (for vol. 2) eu criminal law, policing, and civil law* LCCN: 2016934360 Author/Editor: Peers, Steve. Main title: Eu justice and home affairs law:: (for vol. 1) eu immigration and asylum law (for vol. 2) eu criminal law, policing, and civil law/Steve Peers. Edition: 4th edition. Published/Produced: New York, NY: Oxford University Press, 2016. Description: pages cm ISBN: 9780198776833 (hardback) 9780198776840 (hardback) 9780198776857 (set)

*Experiences of islamophobia: living with racism in the neoliberal era* LCCN: 2015012294 Author/Editor: Carr, James (Sociologist) Main title: Experiences of islamophobia: living with racism in the neoliberal era/James Carr. Published/Produced: New York, NY: Routledge, 2016. Description: xi, 196 pages; 24 cm. ISBN: 9781138851757 (hardback) LC classification: BP52 .C37 2016 Contents: Introduction -- Conducting "race" in a neoliberal world -- De-constructing islamophobia -- Measuring anti-muslim racism: Ireland and abroad -- Conducting hearts and minds: anti-muslim racism in a neoliberal state -- Neoliberal governmentalities of "care": rhetoric and anti-muslim racism in Ireland -- Janus turned: (counter)productive policing -- Opportunities for positive change in the recording and reporting of anti-muslim racism in neoliberal Ireland -- Conclusion -- Appendix 1: Methodology -- Appendix 2: Hate mail sent to muslim communities in Dublin, November 2013 -- Bibliography. Subjects: Islamophobia. Neoliberalism. Notes: Includes bibliographical references (pages 163-190). Series: Routledge research in race and ethnicity

*Faulkner and the black literatures of the Americas: Faulkner and Yoknapatawpha, 2013* LCCN: 2015042215 Meeting name: Faulkner and Yoknapatawpha Conference (40th: 2013: University of Mississippi) Main title: Faulkner and the black literatures of the Americas: Faulkner and Yoknapatawpha, 2013/edited by Jay Watson, James G. Thomas. Published/Produced: Jackson: University Press of Mississippi, 2016. Description: pages cm. Links: Cover image http://www.netread.com/jcusers/1343/3148030/image/lgcover.9781496806345.jpg ISBN: 9781496806345 (hardback) LC classification: PS3511.A86 Z78321137 2013 Authors: Watson, Jay, editor. Thomas, James G., Jr., editor. Summary: "Faulkner and the Black Literatures of the Americas explores relationships between Faulkner's literary oeuvre and a hemispheric canon of black writing from the U.S. and the Caribbean. The volume's seventeen essays and poetry selections chart lines of engagement, dialogue, confluence, and reciprocal resonance between Faulkner and his black precursors, contemporaries, and successors in the Americas"-- Provided by publisher. Contents: Introduction/Jay Watson -- African American Poetic Responses to Faulkner/Chiyuma Elliott, Rachel Eliza Griffiths, Derrick Harriell, Randall Horton, Jamaal May -- The Street Ran through Cities: Faulkner and the Early African American Migration Narrative/James Smethurst -- Lingering in the Black: Faulkner's Illegible Modernist Sound Melding/Thadious M. Davis -- Tracking Faulkner in the Paths of Black Modernism/George Hutchinson -- Miscegenation and Progression: The First Americans of Jean Toomer and William Faulkner/Andrew B. Leiter -- Go to Jail about This Spoonful: Narcotic Determinism and Human Agency in "That Evening Sun" and "A Spoonful Blues"/Tim A. Ryan -- Narrative Leaps to Universal Appeal in McKay's Banjo and Faulkner's A Fable/Dotty Dye -- Reconstructions: Faulkner and Du Bois on the Civil War/T. Austin Graham -- The President Has Asked Me: Faulkner, Ellison, and Public Intellectualism/Joseph Fruscione -- Dangerous Quests: Transgressive Sexualities in William Faulkner's The Wild Palm and James Baldwin's Another Country/Ben Robbins -- From Yoknapatawpha County to St. Raphael Parish: Faulknerian Influence on the Works of Ernest J. Gaines/John Wharton Lowe -- For Fear of a Scandal: Sexual Policing and the Preservation of Colonial Relations in William Faulkner and Marie Vieux-Chauvet/Jenna Sciuto -- In the Book of the Dead, the Narrator Is the Self: Edwidge Danticats The Dew Breaker as a Response to Faulkner's Haiti in

Absalom, Absalom!/Sharron Eve Sarthou -- Contemporary Black Writing and Southern Social Belonging: Beyond the Faulknerian Shadow of Loss/Lisa Hinrichsen -- It Was Enough That the Name Was Written: Ledger Narratives in Edward P. Jones's The Known World and Faulkner's Go Down, Moses/Matthew Dischinger --Morrison's Return to Faulkner: A Mercy and Absalom, Absalom!/Doreen Fowler -- Natasha Trethewey's Joe Christmas and the Reconstruction of Mississippi Nativity/Ted Atkinson. Subjects: Faulkner, William, 1897-1962--Criticism and interpretation--Congresses. Faulkner, William, 1897-1962--Influence--Congresses. Yoknapatawpha County (Imaginary place)--Congresses. American literature--African American authors--History and criticism--Congresses. Caribbean literature (English)--Black authors--History and criticism--Congresses. African Americans in literature--Congresses. Race in literature--Congresses. Literary Criticism/American/General. Literary Collections/American/General. Notes: Papers presented at the fortieth Faulkner and Yoknapatawpha Conference, sponsored by the University of Mississippi, held from July 21-25, 2013. Includes bibliographical references and index. Additional formats: Online version: Faulkner and Yoknapatawpha Conference (40th: 2013: University of Mississippi) Faulkner and the black literatures of the Americas Jackson: University Press of Mississippi, 2016 9781496806352 (DLC) 2016001779 Series: Faulkner and Yoknapatawpha

*Financial crime in China: developments, sanctions, and the systemic spread of corruption* LCCN: 2015020608 Author/Editor: Cheng, Hongming, 1967- Main title: Financial crime in China: developments, sanctions, and the systemic spread of corruption/Hongming Cheng. Published/Produced: New York City, NY: Palgrave Macmillan, 2016. Description: xiv, 194 pages; 23 cm ISBN: 9781137435293 (hardback: alk. paper) LC classification: HV6771.C58 .C44 2016 Contents: The financial system in China: financial sectors, state influences and opportunities for crime -- The upper world -- Banking fraud -- Securities fraud -- Informal finance and ponzi schemes -- Law and the courts -- Policing and regulating financial crime -- Financial business ethics and professionalization in the anomic environment -- Conclusion: financial crime and the "Chinese century." Subjects: Commercial crimes--China. White collar crimes--China. Money laundering--China. Insider trading in securities--Law and legislation--China. Notes: Includes bibliographical references (pages 175-190) and index.

*Gender violence in peace and war: states of complicity* LCCN: 2015047354 Main title: Gender violence in peace and war: states of complicity/edited by Victoria Sanford, Katerina Stefatos, Cecilia M. Salvi. Published/Produced: New Brunswick, New Jersey: Rutgers University Press, 2016. Description: pages cm. ISBN: 9780813576183 (hardcover: alkaline paper) 9780813576176 (paperback: alkaline paper) LC classification: HV6250.4.W65 G477 2016 Authors: Sanford, Victoria. Stefatos, Katerina, 1979- Salvi, Cecilia M., 1987- Scope and content: "A much-needed analysis of the role of the state, its mechanisms and structures in perpetuating, legitimizing and facilitating gender violence worldwide in the first decade and a half of the 21st century. This book documents the nature, extent and progress made in relation to gender-based violence since the advancements in women's rights that had their zenith in the 1990s, and focuses specifically on state participation in and interventions on gender violence. Gender Violence in Peace and War concentrates on gender violence in relation to state practices because, as the chapters clearly demonstrate, sexual victimization, torture, persecution, socioeconomic exclusion and domestic violence fall within the purview of the state and its proxies. Additionally, while gender, violence and the state are frequent and well-analyzed objects of study in social scientific and feminist literature, the full extent of this multilayered relation between all three has not been fully explored in recent social science literature and feminist scholarship in an interdisciplinary context"--Provided by publisher. Contents: Part One. State violence, gender and resistance -- Subaltern bodies: gender violence, sexual torture and political repression during the Greek military dictatorship (1967-1974)/Katerina Stefatos -- Sexual violence as a weapon during the Guatemalan genocide/Victoria Sanford, Sofia Duyos-Álvarez and Kathleen Dill -- Gender, incarceration and power relations during the Irish Civil War (1922-1923)/Laura McAtackney -- Resistance and activism against state violence in Chiapas, Mexico/Melanie Hoewer -- Part Two. The continuum of sexual violence and the role of the state -- Medical record review and evidence of mass rape during the 2007/2008 period of post-election violence in Kenya/Mike Anastario -- The force of writing in genocide: on sexual violence in the al-Anfāl operations and beyond/Fazil Moradi -- Sexualized bodies, public mutilation and torture at the beginning of Indonesia's new order regime (1965-66)/Annie Pohlman -- Part Three. State responses to gender violence -- Advances and limits of policing and human security for women: Nicaragua in comparative perspective/Shannon Drysdale Walsh -- The state to the rescue?: the contested terrain of domestic violence in post-communist Russia/Maija Jäppinen and Janet Elise Johnson -- The absent state: teen mothers and new patriarchal forms of gender subordination/Serena Cosgrove -- Anti-trafficking legislation, gender violence and the state/Cecilia M. Salvi -- Conclusion: Sex at the Security Council: reflections on the women, peace and security agenda/Kimberly Theidon. Subjects: Women--Violence against--Political aspects--History. Sex crimes--Political aspects--History. Political violence--History. Women and war--History. Women's rights--History. Accomplices--Political aspects--History. State, The--History--20th century. State, The--History--21st century. World politics--20th century. World politics--21st century. Notes: Includes bibliographical references and index. Series: Genocide, political violence, human rights series

*Handcuffed: what holds policing back, and the keys to reform* LCCN: 2015040702 Author/Editor: Sparrow, Malcolm K., author. Main title: Handcuffed: what holds policing back, and the keys to reform/Malcolm K. Sparrow. Edition: 1 Edition. Published/Produced: Washington, D.C.: Brookings Institution Press, 2016. Description: pages cm ISBN: 9780815727811 (hardback: alk. paper) LC classification: HV8139 .S6198 2016 Summary: "The police shooting of an unarmed young black man in the St. Louis, Missouri, suburb of Ferguson earlier this year sparked riots and the beginning of a national conversation on race and policing. Much of that conversation has focused more on social issues. Malcolm Sparrow, who teaches at Harvard's Kennedy School and is a former British police detective, argues in this new book that there is another dimension that played a role not only in Ferguson but in many other high-profile police killings of unarmed blacks: the character of policing itself. Sparrow shows how police departments across America have shelved the traditional ideas of community policy-the cop on the beat how knows his or her neighborhood and its inhabitants-and also simple problem solving when it comes to crime to focus on crime reduction. That has meant a reliance on quantitative methods where police define how well they are doing by tallying up how many traffic tickets have been issued (Ferguson), or arrests made for petty crimes (Eric Garner selling nontaxed cigarettes in New York). The list goes on. Police departments need to shed this reliance on crime reduction metrics and mindsets and turn back to making public safety, and public cooperation, their primary goals"-- Provided by publisher. Subjects: Police--United States. Public safety--United States. Race discrimination--United States. Political Science/Political Freedom & Security/Law Enforcement. LAW/Criminal Procedure. Social Science/Discrimination & Race Relations. Political Science/Public Policy/Social Policy. United States--Race relations. Additional formats:

Online version: Sparrow, Malcolm K., author. Handcuffed 1 Edition. Washington, D.C.: Brookings Institution Press, 2016 9780815727828 (DLC) 2016008833

*Hosea Stout: lawman, legislator, Mormon defender* LCCN: 2015033645 Author/Editor: Prince, Stephen L. Main title: Hosea Stout: lawman, legislator, Mormon defender/Stephen Prince. Published/Produced: Logan: Utah State University Press, 2016. Description: pages cm ISBN: 9781607324768 (cloth) LC classification: F826.S76 P75 2016 Scope and content: "Police chief, military officer, city attorney, legislator, and US Attorney, Hosea Stout influenced many of the major civil and political events of LDS and Utah history. He was accused in connection with several deaths and arrested on conspiracy charges in the murder of Richard Yates"-- Provided by publisher. Contents: Shaker education -- Reunion and abandonment -- Quakers and Methodists -- Introduction to Mormonism -- Fight and flight -- Refuge in Illinois -- Rising through the ranks -- Policing Nauvoo -- The trek across Iowa -- Winter quarters -- The pinnacle of violence -- Crossing the plains -- Attorney and legislator -- Mission to China -- Lawyer and legislator -- Reformation and winds of war -- Resisting the feds -- "The attorney of the Mormon Church" -- The Cotton Mission -- Last hurrah -- Epilogue. Subjects: Stout, Hosea, 1810-1889. Mormon pioneers--Utah--Biography. Frontier and pioneer life--Utah. Mormons--Utah--Biography. Legislators--Utah--Biography. Peace officers--Illinois--Nauvoo--Biography. Mormon Church--History--19th century. Utah--History--19th century. Nauvoo (Ill.)--History--19th century. Notes: Includes bibliographical references.

*How the drug war ruins American lives* LCCN: 2015043642 Author/Editor: Benavie, Arthur, author. Main title: How the drug war ruins American lives/Arthur Benavie. Published/Produced: Santa Barbara: Praeger, 2016. Description: pages cm ISBN: 9781440850110 (print: alk. paper) 9781440850127 (ebook) LC classification: HV5825 .B436 2016 Contents: Acknowledgments -- Introduction -- Policing for profit -- The license to steal -- Traffic stops -- Houses arrested -- Swat raids -- Random drug sweeps -- Racial injustice -- Shutting the courthouse door -- Racial disparities -- Police bias in seattle -- Police bias in New York -- Covert operators -- Criminal informants -- Undercover police -- Citizenship barriers -- The criminal population -- Invisible punishments -- Drug testing -- Drug testing students -- Employee drug testing -- Is the war ending? -- Good news! -- The war's beneficiaries -- Summary and conclusions -- Inevitable damages -- Drug war benefits? -- Notes -- Bibliography -- Index. Subjects: Drug control--United States. Drug legalization--United States. Drug testing--United States. Social problems--United States. Notes: Includes bibliographical references and index.

*Human trafficking: the complexities of exploitation* LCCN: 2015510356 Main title: Human trafficking: the complexities of exploitation/edited by Margaret Malloch and Paul Rigby. Published/Produced: Edinburgh: Edinburgh University Press, [2016] Description: ix, 256 pages; 24 cm ISBN: 9781474401128 1474401120 Authors: Malloch, Margaret S., editor. Rigby, Paul, editor. Contents: Contexts and complexities/Margaret Malloch and Paul Rigby -- Productive ignorance: assessing public understanding of human trafficking in Ukraine, Hungary and Great Britain/Kiril Sharapov -- The application of international legislation: is the federalisation of anti-trafficking legislation in Europe working for trafficking victims?/Adam Weiss -- Interantional and European standards in relation to victims and survivors of human victims?/Kirsty Thomson -- Child protection for child trafficking victims/Paul Rigby and Philip Ishola -- Responding to victims of human trafficking: the good, the bad and the ugly/Jim Laird -- Does it happen here?/Sheila Murie and Liz Owens -- Promoting psychological recovery in victims of human trafficking/Sharon Doherty and Rachel Morley -- 'We cannot collect comprehensive information on all these changes': the challenges of monitoring and evaluating reintegration efforts for separated children/Claire Cody -- Policing forced marriages among Pakistanis in the United Kingdom/Stefano Bonino -- Criminalising victims of human trafficking: state responses and punitive practices/Margaret Malloch -- Root causes, transnational mobility and formations of patriarchy in the sex trafficking of women/Jackie Turner -- The new raw resources passing through the shadows/Hazel Cameron -- Human trafficking: capital exploitation and the accursed share/Bill Munro. Subjects: Human trafficking. Notes: Includes bibliographical references and index.

*Incarcerating the crisis: freedom struggles and the rise of the neoliberal state* LCCN: 2015037551 Author/Editor: Camp, Jordan T., 1979- author. Main title: Incarcerating the crisis: freedom struggles and the rise of the neoliberal state/Jordan T. Camp. Published/Produced: Oakland, California: University of California Press, [2016] ©2016 Description: pages cm ISBN: 9780520281813 (cloth: alk. paper) 0520281810 (cloth: alk. paper) 9780520281820 (pbk.: alk. paper) 0520281829 (pbk.: alk. paper) LC classification: HN57 .C33 2016 Summary: “The United States currently has the highest incarceration rate of any country: one in thirty-five adults are in jail, prison, immigrant detention, or on parole or probation. Over the last four decades, structural unemployment, concentrated urban poverty, and mass homelessness have also become permanent features of the political economy. These developments are without historical precedent, but not without historical explanation. In this searing critique, Jordan T. Camp traces the roots of this explosive carceral crisis through a series of turning points in U.S. history including the Watts insurrection in 1965, the Detroit rebellion in 1967, the Attica uprising in 1971, the Los Angeles revolt in 1992, and post-katrina New Orleans in 2005. Incarcerating the Crisis argues that these dramatic events coincided with the emergence of neoliberal capitalism and the state's attempts to crush radical social movements. Through an examination of poetic visions of social movements--including those by James Baldwin, Marvin Gaye, June Jordan, Jose Ramirez, and Sunni Patterson--it also suggests that alternative outcomes have been and continue to be possible."--Provided by publisher. Contents: Introduction: an old world is dying -- The explosion in Watts: The second reconstruction and the cold war roots of the carceral state -- Finally got the news: The black freedom struggle and the crisis of U.S. hegemony in Detroit -- The sound before the fury: Attica, racialized state violence, and the neoliberal turn in New York -- Reading the writing on the wall: The Los Angeles uprising and the Carceral City -- What's going on? Moral panics and militarization in post-Katrina New Orleans -- Shut 'em down: Social movements confront mass homelesness and militarized policing in Los Angeles -- Epilogue: poetry of the future. Subjects: Protest movements--United States--History. Race riots--United States--History. African Americans--Social conditions. Neoliberalism--Social aspects--United States--History. Social problems in mass media. Race relations in mass media. United States--Race relations--History. Notes: Includes bibliographical references and index.

*Indian policing: significance of intelligent leadership* LCCN: 2015515273 Author/Editor: Gahlawat, Dalvir Singh, 1961- author. Main title: Indian policing: significance of intelligent leadership/Dalvir Singh Gahlawat. Published/Produced: New Delhi, India: Authorspress, 2016. Description: 133 pages: illustrations; 23 cm ISBN: 9789352072187 (hardback) 9352072189 (hardback) LC classification: HV8248 (H5)+ Subjects: Police administration--India. Police--India. Notes: Includes bibliographical references and index.

*Intelligence-led policing* LCCN: 2015041681 Author/Editor: Ratcliffe, Jerry, author. Main title: Intelligence-led policing/by Jerry Ratcliffe. Edition: Second Edition. Published/Produced: New York: Routledge, 2016. Description: pages cm ISBN: 9781138858985 (hardback) 9781138859012 (pbk.) LC classification: HV7935 .R37 2016 Contents: Introduction -- Origins of intelligence-led policing -- The magnitude of the crime challenge -- Defining intelligence-led policing -- Police decision-making -- Interpreting the criminal environment -- Influencing decision-makers -- Having an impact on crime -- Technology and ILP -- Evaluating intelligence-led policing -- Challenges for the future. Subjects: Law enforcement. Intelligence service. Crime prevention. Notes: Revision of the author's Intelligence-led policing, 2008. Includes bibliographical references and index.

*Introduction to criminal justice: systems, diversity, and change* LCCN: 2014043875 Author/Editor: Rennison, Callie Marie, author. Main title: Introduction to criminal justice: systems, diversity, and change/Callie Marie Rennison, University of Colorado Denver; Mary Dodge, University of Colorado Denver. Published/Produced: Thousand Oaks, California: SAGE, [2016] Description: xxvii, 401 pages: illustrations (chiefly color); 28 cm ISBN: 9781452240671 (pbk.: alk. paper) LC classification: KF9223 .R46 2016 Authors: Dodge, Mary, 1960- author. Contents: An introduction to crime and the criminal justice system -- The nature and extent of crime -- Criminal justice and the law -- The history of policing -- On the streets: organization, responsibilities, and challenges -- Police and the rule of law -- The courts and judiciary -- The prosecution, defense, and pretrial activities -- The criminal trial and sentencing -- Correctional responses in the community -- Institutional corrections -- Prison life and life after prison --The juvenile justice system -- Exploring specialized and topical issues. Subjects: Criminal justice, Administration of--United States. Crime--United States. Notes: Includes bibliographical references and index.

*Introduction to cybercrime: computer crimes, laws, and policing in the 21st century* LCCN: 2015036592 Author/Editor: Hill, Joshua. Main title: Introduction to cybercrime: computer crimes, laws, and policing in the 21st century/Joshua B. Hill, Nancy E. Marion. Published/Produced: Santa Barbara, CA: Praeger, 2016. Description: 290 pages; 24 cm ISBN: 9781440832734 (hardback) 9781440835339 (paperback) LC classification: HV6773 .H554 2016 Authors: Marion, Nancy E. Summary: "Explaining cybercrime in a highly networked world, this book provides a comprehensive yet accessible summary of the history, modern developments, and efforts to combat cybercrime in various forms at all levels of government--international, national, state, and local. Provides accessible, comprehensive coverage of a complex topic that encompasses identity theft to copyright infringement written for non-technical readers Pays due attention to important elements of cybercrime that have been largely ignored in the field, especially politics Supplies examinations of both the domestic and international efforts to combat cybercrime Serves an ideal text for first-year undergraduate students in criminal justice programs"-- Provided by publisher. Subjects: Computer crimes. Computer crimes--Prevention. Internet--Security measures. Computers/Internet/Security. Law/Communications. Notes: Includes bibliographical references. Series: Praeger security international textbook

*Introduction to policing* LCCN: 2015038734 Author/Editor: Cox, Steven M. Main title: Introduction to policing/Steven M. Cox, Susan Marchionna, Brian D. Fitch. Edition: Third Edition. Published/Produced: Thousand Oaks: SAGE Publications, Inc., 2016. ©2017 Description: pages cm ISBN: 9781506307541 (pbk.: alk. paper) LC classification: HV8139 .C69 2016 Authors: Marchionna, Susan. Fitch, Brian D. Contents: Foundations of policing -- Policing in America -- A brief history of police in the United States -- Police organization and administration: an overview -- Police operations -- Recruitment and selection of police officers -- Police training and education -- Police work: operations and functions -- Contemporary strategies in policing -- Police conduct -- The police culture and work stress -- Law, court decisions, and the police -- Discretion and ethics in policing -- Police misconduct and accountability -- Contemporary issues in policing -- Policing in a diverse society -- Technology and the police -- Transnational crime, white-collar crime, and terrorism -- Private police -- Looking ahead -- The future of policing in america -- . Subjects: Police--United States. Community policing--United States. Notes: Revised edition of Introduction to policing, 2014. Includes bibliographical references and index.

*Introduction to policing research: taking lessons from practice* LCCN: 2015021334 Main title: Introduction to policing research: taking lessons from practice/edited by Mark Brunger, Stephen Tong and Denise Martin. Published/Produced: London; New York: Routledge, 2016. Description: xvi, 230 pages: illustrations; 23 cm ISBN: 9780415750400 (hardback) 9781138013292 (pbk.) LC classification: HV7935 .I58 2016 Authors: Brunger, Mark, editor. Contents: Introduction to policing research/Mark

Brunger, Denise Martin & Steve Tong -- Beyond contrasting traditions in policing research?/Peter Squires -- Policing at a turning point: implications for research/Maurice Punch, Auke van Dijk & Frank Hoogewoning -- Conceptualising private policing/Alison Wakefield -- Policing and mental health/Kristina Massey -- Policing in northern ireland: research, meaning and lessons from a contested landscape/John Topping -- Researching professional development/Dominic Wood & Robin Bryant -- Watching the detectives: researching investigative practice/Katja Hallenburg, Martin O¿Neill & Steve Tong -- Inside policing -- Researching sexual violence/Emma Williams & Betsy Stanko -- From the briefing room to the class room: the pedagogical value of researching police elites/Mark Brunger, Bryn Caless, Steve Tong, & Paul Gilbert -- Policing protest: public order policing/Denise Martin & William Graham -- Outsiders inside: ethnography and police culture/Louise Westmarland -- Researching police diversity/Michael Rowe -- The ethics of researching the police: dilemmas and new directions/Layla Skinns, Andrew Wooff & Amy Sprawson -- Researching sexuality and policing: reflections from the field/Matthew Jones -- Conclusion: challenges and changes in police research/Denise Martin & Steve Tong. Subjects: Police--Research. Notes: Includes bibliographical references and index.

*Law, justice, and society: a sociolegal introduction* LCCN: 2015049374 Author/Editor: Walsh, Anthony, 1941- author. Main title: Law, justice, and society: a sociolegal introduction/Anthony Walsh, Boise State University; Craig Hemmens, Washington State University. Edition: Fourth edition. Published/Produced: New York: Oxford University Press, 2016. Description: pages cm ISBN: 9780190272753 (alk. paper) LC classification: KF386 .W325 2016 Authors: Hemmens, Craig, author. Contents: Law: its function and purpose -- Justice and the law -- Making law -- Federal and state courts -- Crime and criminal law -- Criminal procedure -- Civil and administrative law -- Juvenile justice -- The law and social control -- The limits of social control: policing vice -- Law, social change, and the class struggle -- Women and the law/by Mary K. Stohr -- Racial minorities and the law -- Comparative law: law in other countries. Subjects: Law--Social aspects--United States. Justice, Administration of--United States. Sociological jurisprudence. Form/Genre: Textbooks. Additional formats: Online version: Walsh, Anthony, 1941- author. Law, justice, and society Fourth edition. New York: Oxford University Press, 2016 9780190610418 (DLC) 2015050025

*Living in the Ottoman realm: empire and identity, 13th to 20th centuries* LCCN: 2016008081 Main title: Living in the Ottoman realm: empire and identity, 13th to 20th centuries/edited by Christine Isom-Verhaaren and Kent F. Schull. Published/Produced: Bloomington: Indiana University Press, 2016. Description: pages cm ISBN: 9780253019301 (cloth: alkaline paper) 9780253019431 (paperback: alkaline paper) LC classification: DR486 .L58 2016 Authors: Isom-Verhaaren, Christine. Schull, Kent F. Scope and content: "Living in the Ottoman Realm brings the Ottoman Empire to life in all of its ethnic, religious, linguistic, and geographic diversity. The contributors explore the development and transformation of identity over the long span of the empire's existence. They offer engaging accounts of individuals, groups, and communities by drawing on a rich array of primary sources, some available in English translation for the first time. These materials are examined with new methodological approaches to gain a deeper understanding of what it meant to be Ottoman. Designed for use as a course text, each chapter includes study questions and suggestions for further reading"--Provided by publisher. Contents: Introduction: Dealing with identity in the Ottoman Empire/Christine Isom-Verhaaren and Kent F. Schull -- Part I. 13th through 15th centuries--Emergence and expansion: from frontier Beylik to cosmopolitan empire -- The giving divide: food gifts and social identity in late medieval Anatolia/Nicolas Trepanier -- Changing perceptions along the frontiers: the moving frontier with rum in late medieval Anatolian frontier narratives/Zeynep Aydogan -- The Genoese of Pera in the fifteenth century: Draperio and Spinola families/F. Ozden Mercan -- From Byzantine aristocracy to Ottoman ruling elite: Mahmud Pasha Angelovic and his Christian circle, 1458-1474/Theoharis Stavrides -- Interpreting Ottoman identity with the historian Nesri Murat Cem Menguc -- A shaykh, a prince, and a sack of corn: an Anatolian Sufi becomes Ottoman/Hasan Karatas -- Part II. 15th through 17th centuries--Expansion and cultural splendor: the creation of a Sunni Islamic empire -- Ibn-i Kemal's confessionalism and the construction of an Ottoman Islam/Nabil Al-Tikriti -- Becoming Ottoman in sixteenth-century Aintab/Leslie Peirce -- Making Jerusalem Ottoman/Amy Singer -- Ibrahim ibn Khidr al-Qaramani: a merchant and urban notable of early Ottoman Aleppo/Charles Wilkins -- Mihrimah Sultan: a princess constructs Ottoman dynastic identity/Christine -- Isom-Verhaaren -- Part III. 17th through 18th centuries--Upheaval and transformation: from conquest to administrative state -- The Sultan's advisors and their opinions on the identity of the Ottoman elite, 1580-1653/Linda T. Darling -- Fleeing "the vomit of infidelity": borders, conversion, and Muslim women's agency/Eric Dursteler -- Policing morality: crossing gender and communal boundaries in an age of political crisis and religious controversy/Fariba Zarinebaf -- Leaving France, "turning Turk," becoming Ottoman: the transformation of Comte Claude-Alexandre de Bonneval into Humbaraci Ahmed Pasha/Julia Landweber -- Out of Africa, into the palace: the Ottoman chief harem eunuch/Jane Hathaway -- The province goes to the center: the case of Hadjiyorgakis Kornesios, Dragoman of Cyprus/Antonis Hadjikyriacou -- Part IV. 19th through 20th centuries--Modernity, mass politics, and nationalism: from empire to nation-state -- Ruler visibility, modernity, and ethnonationalism in the late Ottoman Empire/Darin N. Stephanov -- Muslims' contributions to science and Ottoman identity/M. Alper Yalcinkaya -- Migrants, revolutionaries, and spies: surveillance, politics, and Ottoman identity in the United States/David Gutman -- A Cappadocian in Athens, an Athenian in Smyrna, and a Parliamentarian in Istanbul: the multiple personae and loyalties of Pavlos Carolidis/Vangelis Kechriotis -- Zionism in the era of Ottoman brotherhood/Michelle U. Campos -- Connections and questions to consider. Subjects: Cultural pluralism--Turkey--History. Imperialism--Social aspects--Turkey--History. Identity (Psychology)--Turkey--History. Group identity--Turkey--History. Ethnicity--Turkey--History. Community life--Turkey--History. Social change--Turkey--History. Turkey--History--Ottoman Empire, 1288-1918. Turkey--Social conditions--1288-1918. Turkey--Ethnic relations--History. Notes: Includes bibliographical references and index. Additional formats: Online version: Living in the Ottoman realm Bloomington: Indiana University Press, 2016 9780253019486 (DLC) 2016009336

*On marronage: ethical confrontations with antiblackness* LCCN: 2015031580 Main title: On marronage: ethical confrontations with antiblackness/edited by P. Khalil Saucier and Tryon P. Woods. Edition: 1 Edition. Published/Produced: Trenton: Africa World Press, 2016. Description: pages cm ISBN: 9781569024539 (alk. paper) LC classification: E184.7 .O5 2016 Authors: Saucier, Paul Khalil, 1976- editor. Woods, Tryon P. Contents: Acknowledgments -- What is the danger in black studies and can we look at it again (and again)?/P. Khalil Saucier and Tryon P. Woods -- Afrarealism and the black matrix: maroon philosophy at democracy's border/Joy James -- Venus in two acts/Saidiya Hartman -- The body politics of "man" and "woman" in an "anti-black" world: sylvia wynter on humanism's empire (a critical resource guide)/Greg Thomas -- Saving mr. jefferson: slavery and denial at monticello/Kimberly Juanita Brown -- Scenes/Christina Sharpe -- Against hip hop studies/P. Khalil Saucier & Tryon P. Woods -- Precarity as capture: a conceptual deconstruction of the worker-slave analogy/Franco Barchiesi -- The vengeance of vertigo: aphasia and abjection in the political trials of black insurgents/Frank B. Wilderson, III -- A re-appraisal of black radicalism and human rights doctrine/Tryon P. Woods -- Proprieties of coalition: blacks, asians, and the politics of policing/Jared Sexton -- List of contributors. Subjects: African Americans--Study and teaching--United States. Blacks--Study and teaching--United States. Racism in popular culture--United States. Maroons--United States. Prejudices--United States.

*Pioneering healthcare law: essays in honour of Margaret Brazier* LCCN: 2015020094 Main title: Pioneering healthcare law: essays in honour of Margaret Brazier/edited by Catherine Stanton, Sarah Devaney, Anne-Maree Farrell and Alexandra Mullock. Published/Produced: Milton Park, Abingdon, Oxon; New York, NY: Routledge, 2016. Description: xxvi, 308 pages; 24 cm. ISBN: 9781138861091 (hbk) LC classification: K3601 .P56 2016 Authors: Stanton, Catherine (Law teacher) editor. Devaney, Sarah, editor. Farrell, Anne-Maree, 1964- editor. Mullock, Alexandra, editor. Brazier, Margaret, honouree. Contents: Pioneering healthcare law/Anne-Maree Farrell, Catherine Stanton, Alexandra Mullock, Sarah Devaney -- Waxing and waning: the shifting sands of autonomy on the medico-legal shore/Graeme T. Laurie, J. Kenyon Mason -- Compulsory vaccination: going beyond a civic duty?/Nicola Glover-Thomas & Søren Holm -- The value of human life in healthcare law: life versus death in the hands of the judiciary/Alexandra Mullock and Rob Heywood -- Decisions at the end of life: an attempt at rationalisation/Sheila A.M. McLean -- The past, present and future of EU health law/Tamara Hervey -- Beyond medicine, patients and the law: policy and governance in 21st century health law/John Coggon and Lawrence O Gostin -- (I love you!) I do, I do, I do, I do, I do: breaches of sexual boundaries by patients in their relationships with healthcare professionals/Hazel Biggs and Suzanne Ost -- When things go wrong: patient harm, responsibility and (dis)empowerment/Anne-Maree Farrell and Sarah Devaney -- Critical decisions for critically ill infants: principles, processes, problems/Giles Birchley and Richard Huxtable -- The role of the family in healthcare decisions: the dead and the dying/Monica Navarro-Michel -- Exploring the legacy of the retained organs commission a decade on: lessons learned and the danger of lessons lost/Jean V McHale -- Property interests in human tissue: is the law still an ass?/Muireann Quigley and Loane Skene -- Law and humanity: exploring organ donation using the Brazier method/Marleen Eijkholt and Ruth Stirton -- Sex change surgery for transgender minors: should doctors speak out?/Simona Giordano, César Palacios-González and John Harris -- The lawyer's prestige/Iain Brassington and Imogen Jones -- The science of muddling through: categorising embryos/Marie Fox and Sheelagh McGuinness -- Revisiting the regulation of the reproduction business/Danielle Griffiths and Amel Alghrani -- Regulating responsible reproduction/David Archard -- Donor conception and information disclosure: welfare or consent?/Rosamund Scott -- Are we still "policing pregnancy"?/Sara Fovargue and Jose Miola -- Vulnerability and the criminal law: the implications of Brazier's research for safeguarding people at risk/Kirsty Keywood and Zuzanna Sawicka -- Revisiting the criminal law on the transmission of disease/David Gurnham and Andrew Ashworth -- Maternal responsibility to the child not yet born/Emma Cave and Catherine Stanton -- Compromise medicalisation/Roger Brownsword and Jeffrey Wale. Subjects: Medical laws and legislation. Medical laws and legislation--Great Britain. Series: Biomedical law and ethics library

*Policing and social media: social control in an era of new media* LCCN: 2016000115 Author/Editor: Schneider, Christopher J., author. Main title: Policing and social media: social control in an era of new media/by Christopher J. Schneider. Published/Produced: Lanham: Lexington Books, [2016] Description: pages cm ISBN: 9781498533713 (cloth: alk. paper) 9781498533737 (pbk.: alk. paper) LC classification: HV7936.P8 S38 2016 Contents: Introduction: media logic, policing, and social media -- Media formats and police social control practices -- Crime and society 2.0: police and social networking -- Facebook and the 2011 Vancouver riot -- Police presentational strategies on Twitter -- Police caught on camera: framing the death of Sammy Yatim -- Conclusion: policing on social media. Subjects: Police-community relations--Canada. Police misconduct--Canada. Social media--Canada. Police and mass media--Canada. Mass media and criminal justice--Canada. Notes: Includes bibliographical references and index. Additional formats: Online version: Schneider, Christopher J., author. Policing and social media Lanham: Lexington Books, [2016] 9781498533720 (DLC) 2016008835

*Policing immigrants: local law enforcement on the front lines* LCCN: 2015041262 Author/Editor: Provine, Doris Marie, author. Main title: Policing immigrants: local law enforcement on the front lines/Doris Marie Provine, Monica W. Varsanyi, Paul G. Lewis, and Scott H. Decker. Published/Produced: Chicago: The University of Chicago Press, 2016.

Description: pages; cm. ISBN: 9780226363042 (cloth: alk. paper) 9780226363189 (pbk.: alk. paper) LC classification: JV6483 .P77 2016 Authors: Varsanyi, Monica, 1971- author. Lewis, Paul George, 1966- author. Decker, Scott H., author. Contents: Introducing the conflicted politics of localized immigration control -- The evolution of devolution -- The problematic patchwork of immigration federalism -- Going their own way: community context and its influences on the patchwork -- Discretion on the front lines: immigrant policing in action -- Negotiated understandings between law enforcement and local communities -- Conclusions and recommendations: finding the way forward. Subjects: Immigration enforcement--United States. Central-local government relations--United States. Immigrants--Legal status, laws, etc.--United States. United States--Emigration and immigration--Government policy. Notes: Includes bibliographical references and index. Series: Chicago series in law and society Chicago series in law and society.

*Policing in Israel: studying crime control, community policing, and counterterrorism* LCCN: 2015013763 Main title: Policing in Israel: studying crime control, community policing, and counterterrorism/edited by Tal Jonathan-Zamir, The Hebrew University of Jerusalem, Jerusalem Israel; David Weisburd, The Hebrew University of Jerusalem, Jerusalem Israel [and] George Mason University, Fairfax, Virginia, USA; Badi Hasisi, The Hebrew University of Jerusalem, Jerusalem Israel. Published/Produced: Boca Raton: CRC Press, Taylor & Francis Group, [2016] Description: xiv, 262 pages: maps, charts; 27 cm. ISBN: 9781498722568 LC classification: HV8242.2.A3 P65 2016 Authors: Jonathan-Zamir, Tal, editor. Weisburd, David, editor. Hasisi, Badi, editor. Contents: Policing in Israel: Studying Crime Control, Community, and Counterterrorism: Editors' Introduction/Tal Jonathan-Zamir, David Weisburd, and Badi Hasisi -- Law of Concentrations of Crime at Place: Case of Tel Aviv-Jaffa/David Weisburd and Shai Amram -- Vehicle Impoundment Regulations as a Means of Reducing Traffic Violations and Road Accidents in Israel/Tova Rosenbloom and Ehud Eldror -- Lean Management for Traffic Police Enforcement Planning/Nicole Adler, Jonathan Kornbluth, Mali Sher, and Shalom Hakkert -- Organizational Structure, Police Activity, and Crime/Itai Ater, Yehonatan Givati, and Oren Rigbi -- Police, Politics, and Culture in a Deeply Divided Society/Badi Hasisi -- Crime Victims and Attitudes toward Police: Israeli Case/Gali Aviv -- Procedural Justice, Minorities, and Religiosity/Roni Factor, Juan Castilo, and Arye Rattner -- Police Understanding of Foundations of Their Legitimacy in the Eyes of the Public: Case of Commanding Officers in Israel National Police/Tal

Jonathan-Zamir and Amikam Harpaz -- Terrorist Threats and Police Performance: A Study of Israeli Communities/David Weisburd, Badi Hasisi, Tal Jonathan-Zamir, and Gali Aviv -- Police Legitimacy under the Spotlight: Media Coverage of Police Performance in the Face of High Terrorism Threat/Revital Sela-Shayovitz -- Policing Terrorism and Police-Community Relations: Views of Arab Minority in Israel/Badi Hasisi and David Weisburd -- How Has Israel National Police Perceived Its Role in Counterterrorism and Potential Outcomes?: A Qualitative Analysis of Annual Police Reports/Tal Jonathan-Zamir and Gali Aviv -- Lessons from Empirical Research on Policing in Israel: Policing Terrorism and Police-Community Relationships/Simon Perry and Tal Jonathan-Zamir. Subjects: Police--Israel. Law enforcement--Israel. Notes: Includes bibliographical references and index. Series: Advances in police theory and practice series

*Policing* LCCN: 2014035222 Author/Editor: Worrall, John L. Main title: Policing/John L. Worrall; Professor of Criminology, University of Texas at Dallas, Frank Schmalleger, Distinguished Professor Emeritus, University of North Carolina at Pembroke. Edition: Second edition. Published/Produced: Boston: Pearson, [2016] Description: xv, 272 pages; 28 cm ISBN: 9780133587586 (alk. paper) 0133587584 (alk. paper) LC classification: HV8139 .W67 2016 Contents: Origins and evolution of American policing -- Policing in American context -- Law enforcement agencies and their organization -- Becoming a cop -- Police subculture -- Police discretion and behavior -- Core police functions -- Community policing and community involvement -- Policing in the modern era -- Policing and the law -- Civil liability and accountability -- Deviance, ethics, and professionalism -- The use of force. Subjects: Police--United States. Law enforcement--United States. Criminal justice, Administration of--United States. Notes: Includes bibliographical references (pages 231-252) and indexes.

*Policing the planet: why the policing crisis led to black lives matter* LCCN: 2016007516 Main title: Policing the planet: why the policing crisis led to black lives matter/edited by Jordan T. Camp, Christina Heatherton. Published/Produced: New York: Verso, 2016. Description: pages cm ISBN: 9781784783167 (paperback) LC classification: HV8141 .P5977 2016 Authors: Camp, Jordan T., 1979- editor. Heatherton, Christina, editor. Summary: “A probing collection of essays and interviews addressing police brutality and racial injustice Policing has become one of the urgent issues of our time, the target of dramatic movements and front-page coverage from coast to coast in the United States and across the world. Now a wide-ranging collection of writers and activists offers a global response, describing ongoing struggles from New York to Ferguson to Los Angeles, as well as London, San Juan, San Salvador, and beyond. This book, combining first-hand accounts from organizers with the interventions of scholars and contributions by leading artists, traces the global rise of the "broken-windows" strategy of policing, first established in New York City under Police Commissioner William Bratton, a doctrine that has vastly broadened police power and contributed to the contemporary crisis of policing that has been sparked by notorious incidents of police brutality and killings. With contributions from #BlackLivesMatter cofounder Patrisse Cullors, Ferguson activist and St. Louis University law professor Justin Hansford, poet Martín Espada, scholars Ruth Wilson Gilmore, Robin D.G. Kelley, Naomi Murakawa, Vijay Prashad, and many more"-- Provided by publisher. Subjects: Police brutality--United States. Discrimination in law enforcement--United States. Police--Complaints against--United States. Police-community relations--United States. Social Science/Sociology/Urban. LAW/Civil Rights. Political Science/Political Freedom & Security/Civil Rights.

*Policing, port security and crime control: an ethnography of the port securityscape* LCCN: 2015050292 Author/Editor: Eski, Yarin. Main title: Policing, port security and crime control: an ethnography of the port securityscape/Yarin Eski. Edition: First Edition. Published/Produced: New York: Routledge, 2016. Description: pages cm. ISBN: 9781138639461 (hardback) LC classification: HE551 .E85 2016 Contents: An ethnographic approach -- Imagining the port securityscape -- Management, colleagues and partners -- The port business community -- The shipping industry -- Stowaways, port thieves and drug smugglers -- Terrorists -- Conclusion. Subjects: Harbors--Security measures. Crime prevention. Community policing. Notes: Includes bibliographical references and index. Series: Routledge studies in crime and society; 21

*Predator empire: drone warfare and full spectrum dominance* LCCN: 2015036890 Author/Editor: Shaw, Ian G. R. Main title: Predator empire: drone warfare and full spectrum dominance/Ian G.R. Shaw. Published/Produced: Minneapolis: University of Minnesota Press, [2016] Description: pages cm ISBN: 9780816694730 (hc: alk. paper) 9780816694747 (pb: alk. paper) LC classification: UA23 .S464 2016 Portion of title: Drone warfare and full spectrum dominance Contents: Introduction: understanding empire -- The long march to human enclosure -- The rise of the Predator Empire in the Vietnam War -- Full-spectrum global dominance -- The rule by nobody -- Policing everything -- Conclusion: the war of all against all. Subjects: Military art and science--Technological innovations--Social aspects. Drone aircraft--United States--Social aspects. Targeted killing--United States--Social aspects. National security--United States. Terrorism--Government policy--United States. Hegemony--United States. Social control. Police--United States. Technology and civilization. United States--Military policy. Notes: Includes bibliographical references and index.

*Race, ethnicity, crime & justice* LCCN: 2015025603 Main title: Race, ethnicity, crime & justice/edited by Matthew B. Robinson. Published/Produced: Durham: Carolina Academic Press, 2016. Description: xvi, 317 pages; 23 cm ISBN: 9781611636376 (alk. paper) LC classification: HV9960.U55 R33 2016 Authors: Robinson, Matthew B., editor. Contents: Preface -- Introduction to race and ethnicity/by Matthew Robinson -- Introduction to criminal and juvenile justice/by Beverly Crank -- How race and ethnicity impact the criminal law/by Matthew Robinson -- Relationships between race, ethnicity and crime/by Catherine D. Marcum and Bethany Poff -- Policing in a multicultural society/by Tammatha Clodfelter and Matthew Robinson -- The courts in a color-blind society/by Marian Williams -- How race and ethnicity impact criminal sentencing/by Rhys Hester -- Race, ethnicity, and corrections/by Barbara H. Zaitzow -- Race, ethnicity, and the death penalty in America/by Jefferson Holcomb -- Race, ethnicity, and juvenile justice/by Jason Williams -- Summary and the future/by Matthew Robinson. Subjects: Crime and race--United States. Discrimination in criminal justice administration--United States. Criminal justice, Administration of--United States. Notes: Includes bibliographical references and index.

*Radiation brain moms and citizen scientists: the gender politics of food contamination after the Fukushima* LCCN: 2016008607 Author/Editor: Kimura, Aya Hirata, 1974- author. Main title: Radiation brain moms and citizen scientists: the gender politics of food contamination after the Fukushima/Aya Hirata Kimura. Published/Produced: Durham: Duke University Press, 2016. Description: pages cm ISBN: 9780822361824 (hardcover: alk. paper) 9780822361992 (pbk.: alk. paper) LC classification: HV623 2011.F85 K56 2016 Contents: “Moms with radiation brain”: gendered food policing in the name of science -- Engineering citizens -- School lunches: science, motherhood, and joshi power -- Citizen radiation-measuring organizations -- The temporality of contaminants. Subjects: Fukushima Nuclear Disaster, Japan, 2011. Food contamination--Japan. Mothers--Japan. Japan--Social conditions--21st century. Notes: Includes bibliographical references and index. Additional formats: Online version: Kimura, Aya Hirata, 1974- author. Radiation brain moms and citizen scientists Durham: Duke University Press, 2016 9780822373964 (DLC) 2016011248

*Rural crime and community safety* LCCN: 2015004168 Author/Editor: Ceccato, Vania. Main title: Rural crime and community safety/Vania Ceccato. Edition: First Edition. Published/Produced: New York, NY: Routledge, 2016. Description: xxx, 394 pages; 24 cm. ISBN: 9780415856430 (hardback) LC classification: HV6791 .C43 2016 Contents: Introduction -- Aim, scope and book structure -- Crime and safety in rural areas -- Definitions, theory, and research making -- Trends and patterns of crime -- Rural-urban crime trends in an international perspective -- The geography of property and violent crime in sweden -- Perceived safety in rural areas -- The nature of perceived safety in rural areas -- Perceived safety in swedish rural areas -- Crime in a rural context -- Farm crimes and environmental and wildlife offences -- Youth in rural areas -- Violence against women in rural communities -- Policing and crime prevention in rural Sweden -- Police, rural policing and community safety -- Prevention of farm crimes and crimes against nature -- Crime prevention in rural areas: youth-related challenges -- Challenges to preventing women abuse in rural communities -- The difference that rural makes -- Lessons from rural Sweden and looking ahead. Subjects: Rural crimes. Women--Crimes against--Sweden--Case studies. Crime prevention--Sweden--Case studies. Series: Routledge studies in crime and society; 18

*Sex crime* LCCN: 2015017529 Author/Editor: Thomas, Terry, 1946- Main title: Sex crime/Terry Thomas. Edition: Third Edition. Published/Produced: Abingdon, Oxon; New York: Routledge, 2016. Description: xi, 259 pages; 25 cm ISBN: 9781138019447 (hardback) 9781138019454 (pbk.) LC classification: HV6593.G7 T56 2016 Contents: Introduction -- The sex offender "problem" and responses -- Social responses to the sex offender: a historical perspective -- Policing sexual offending -- The search for justice: the sex offender in court -- The search for justice: punishing the sex offender -- The victims of sexual offending -- Protection in the home -- Protection in the community -- Conclusions. Subjects: Sex crimes--Great Britain. Notes: Revised edition of the author's Sex crime, 2005. Includes bibliographical references and index.

*Sex testing: gender policing in women's sports* LCCN: 2015042892 Author/Editor: Pieper, Lindsay Parks, 1985- author. Main title: Sex testing: gender policing in women's sports/Lindsay Parks Pieper. Published/Produced: Urbana: University of Illinois Press, 2016. Description: pages cm. ISBN: 9780252040221 (hardback) 9780252081682 (paperback) LC classification: GV709 .P48 2016 Summary: "In 1968, the International Olympic Committee (IOC) implemented sex testing for female athletes at that year's Games. When it became clear that testing regimes failed to delineate a sex divide, the IOC began to test for gender --a shift that allowed the organization to control the very idea of womanhood. Lindsay Parks Pieper explores sex testing in sport from the 1930s to the early 2000s. Focusing on assumptions and goals as well as means, Pieper examines how the IOC in particular insisted on a misguided binary notion of gender that privileged Western norms. Testing evolved into a tool to identify--and eliminate--athletes the IOC deemed too strong, too fast, or too successful. Pieper shows how this system punished gifted women while hindering the development of women's athletics for decades. She also reveals how the flawed notions behind testing--ideas often sexist, racist, or ridiculous--degraded the very idea of female athleticism"-- Provided by publisher. "To assess the long-lasting significance of sex testing in sport, this book explores its history, from the 1930s to the early 2000s, with particular emphasis on the International Olympic Committee's mandated compulsory sex checks on all female competitors. In 1968 the Medical Commission implemented the first test of the modern Olympic Movement. The procedure intended to guarantee the authenticity of Olympic competitors and identify male masqueraders, as well as to scientifically confirm the separation of men and women in athletic competition. Although the Medical Commission never discovered a single male imposter, and the test illustrated the impossibility of determining the exact constitution of woman, the IOC maintained the policy for three decades. With both the impossibility of discovering a clear sex divide and the increased presence of female dopers, the IOC adjusted its semantic framework to encapsulate gender normativity. The conspicuous adjustment from sex to gender underscored the Medical Commission's changing anxieties. Rather than to catch men disguised as women, the test evolved into a measure to preclude female Olympians with biological advantages. In other words, the Medical Commission eventually viewed gender verification as a tool to eliminate competitors it deemed too strong, too fast or too successful for women's competition. Olympic womanhood--dependent on a belief in natural, dichotomous sex/gender difference--required female athletes to conform to conventional notions of white, Western femininity. Through these regulations, the IOC has continuously reaffirmed a binary notion of sex, privileged white gender norms and hampered female athleticism"-- Provided by publisher. Subjects: IOC Medical Commission. Women athletes--Physiology. Sex discrimination in sports. Sports--Sex differences. Social Science/Gender Studies. Social Science/Women's Studies. Sports & Recreation/Olympics. Notes: Includes bibliographical references and index. Additional formats: Online version: Pieper, Lindsay Parks, 1985- author. Sex testing Urbana: University of Illinois Press, 2016 9780252098444 (DLC) 2016004102 Series: Sport and society

*State terror, state violence: global perspectives* LCCN: 2015512445 Main title: State terror, state violence: global perspectives/Bettina Koch, editor. Published/Produced: Wiesbaden: Springer VS, [2016] Description: vii, 170 pages; 21 cm. ISBN: 9783658111809 3658111801 Authors: Koch, Bettina, 1970- editor. Contents: Terror, violence, coercion: states and the use of (il)legitimate force/Bettina Koch -- International law and the use of armed force by states/Abel S. Knottnerus -- Securitization and terroristization: analyzing states' usage of the rhetoric of terrorism/Priya Dixit -- From colonialism to globalization: state violence in modern India/Eva-Maria Nag -- Violence on the periphery of the Thai state and nationhood/Karin Zackari -- Violence from above, violence from below: the state and policing citizens in Mubarak's Egypt/Dina Rashed -- Killing the chicken to scare the monkey: some notes on state terror in the People's Republic of China/Peter R. Moody -- Violence by proxy: state-sponsored rebels and criminals in Chechnya/Yelena Biberman -- U.S.-drones strikes: acts of terror, violence, or coercion?/Bettina Koch. Subjects: State-sponsored terrorism. Political violence. Violence--Government policy. Notes: Includes bibliographical references. Additional formats: 9783658111816 (GyWOH)har165000395 Series: Staat--Souveränität--Nation.

*The autonomy of pleasure: libertines, license, and sexual revolution* LCCN: 2015013320 Author/Editor: Steintrager, James A., 1965- Main title: The autonomy of pleasure: libertines, license, and sexual revolution/James A. Steintrager. Published/Produced: New York: Columbia University Press, [2016] Description: xi, 394 pages: illustrations; 24 cm. ISBN: 9780231151580 (cloth: alk. paper) LC classification: HQ18.F8 S74 2016 Contents: Acknowledgments -- Introduction: whose sexual revolution? -- A thousand modes of venery: coital positions as actions and communications -- Voluptuary architecture: organizing, policing, and producing pleasure --

Sodomy and reason: making sense of the libertine preference -- "The obscene organ of brute pleasure": social functions of the clitoris -- The fury of her kindness: what should a libertine know about orgasm? -- Color and caprice: the politics and aesthetics of interracial relations -- Canonizing Sade: eros, democracy, and differentiation -- Notes -- Index. Subjects: Sex customs--France--History--18th century. France--Moral conditions. Notes: Includes bibliographical references (pages 299-376) and index. Series: Columbia themes in philosophy, social criticism, and the arts

*The global making of policing: postcolonial perspectives* LCCN: 2016002109 Main title: The global making of policing: postcolonial perspectives/edited by Jana Hönke and Markus-Michael Müller Published/Produced: Abingdon, Oxon; New York, NY: Routledge, 2016. Description: pages cm. ISBN: 9781138910201 (hardback) LC classification: HV7921 .G584 2016 Authors: Hönke, Jana, editor. Müller, Markus M., editor. Subjects: Police. Internal security. Security, International. Postcolonialism. Notes: Includes bibliographical references and index. Series: Interventions

*The integrity of criminal process: from theory into practice* LCCN: 2016015043 Main title: The integrity of criminal process: from theory into practice/edited by Jill Hunter, Paul Roberts, Simon NM Young, and David Dixon. Published/Produced: Oxford; Portland, Oregon: Hart Publishing Ltd, an imprint of Bloomsbury Publishing Plc, 2016. Description: pages cm ISBN: 9781849465946 (hardback: alk. paper) LC classification: K5001.A6 I58 2016 Authors: Hunter, Jill B., editor. Roberts, Paul, 1968- editor. Young, Simon N. M., editor. Dixon, David, 1954 June 21- editor. University of Hong Kong. Faculty of Law, sponsoring body. University of New South Wales. Faculty of Law, sponsoring body. University of Nottingham. School of Law, sponsoring body. Contents: Introduction: re-examining criminal process through the lens of integrity/Paul Roberts, Jill Hunter, Simon NM Young and David Dixon -- A public law conception of integrity in the criminal process/Simon NM Young -- Searching for integrity in domestic violence policing/Julie Stubbs -- Integrity, interrogation and criminal injustice/David Dixon -- Factory farming and state-induced pleas/Mike McConville and Luke Marsh -- Negotiating justice with integrity in new south wales/Nicholas Cowdery -- The integrity of charging decisions/Jeremy Gans -- Prosecutors interviewing witnesses: a question of integrity/Paul Roberts -- Integrity, immunity and accomplice witness testimony/Michael I Jackson -- Expert evidence and the responsibilities of prosecutors/Gary Edmond -- Stays of prosecution and remedial integrity/Amanda Whitfort -- Excluding integrity?: revisiting non-consequentialist justifications for excluding improperly obtained evidence in criminal trials/Peter Chau -- Unbecoming jurors and unreasoned verdicts: realising integrity in the jury room/John Jackson -- Remorse and demeanour in the courtroom: cognitive science and the evaluation of contrition/Susan A Bandes -- Rape law, past wrongs and legal fictions: telling law's story with integrity/Jill Hunter -- Against innocence/Charles D Weisselberg -- Compensating injustice: the perils of the innocence discourse/Carolyn Hoyle. Subjects: Criminal justice, Administration of--Congresses. Notes: Includes papers presented at linked workshops “Conduct Unbecoming: Realising Integrity in Criminal Justice” at the University of Hong Kong Faculty of Law's Centre for Comparative and Public Law in December 2012, and “Realising Integrity in Criminal Justice” at the University of New South Wales Faculty of Law, Sydney, in April 2013.”--ECIP Acknowledgements. Includes bibliographical references and index. Additional formats: Online version: Integrity of criminal process Oxford; Portland, Oregon: Hart Publishing Ltd, an imprint of Bloomsbury Publishing Plc, 2016 9781782255727 (DLC) 2016015642

*The power of the prosecutor: gatekeepers of the criminal justice system* LCCN: 2015029438 Author/Editor: Jacoby, Joan E., author. Main title: The power of the prosecutor: gatekeepers of the criminal justice system/Joan E. Jacoby, Edward C. Ratledge. Published/Produced: Santa Barbara, California: Praeger, an imprint of ABC-CLIO, LLC [2016] Description: xiii, 227 pages; 25 cm ISBN: 9781440842184 (hardback) LC classification: KF9640 .J288 2016 Authors: Ratledge, Edward C., author. Contents: What is discretion and why do we care? -- Discretion and policing -- Controlling the gate to the courts -- The final accounting: from filing to disposition -- Falling apart -- Dsk: a rush to judgement -- The duke lacrosse players: prosecutorial misconduct -- JonBenet Ramsey: the case that never was -- Casey Anthony: truth and consequences -- Orenthal James Simpson: the murder trial of a victim? -- Professionalism and innovation -- Lessons learned. Subjects: Prosecution--United States. LAW/Criminal Procedure. Law/Criminal Law/General. Notes: Includes bibliographical references (pages 215-219) and index.

*The psychology of crime, policing and courts* LCCN: 2015045847 Main title: The psychology of crime, policing and courts/edited by Andreas Kapardis and David Farrington. Edition: First Edition. Published/Produced: New York, NY: Routledge, 2016. Description: pages cm. ISBN:

9781138931213 (hardback) LC classification: HV6080 .P837 2016 Authors: Kapardis, Andreas, editor. Farrington, David P., editor. Contents: Foreword/Ray Bull -- Introduction: psychology, crime, policing and courts/Andreas Kapardis and David P. Farrington -- Crime and antisocial behaviour -- The concentration of convictions in two generations of families/David P. Farrington and Rebecca V. Crago -- Self-reported juvenile delinquency in three surveys over 38 years: a german study on the crime drop/Friedrich Lösel, Doris Bender, Zara Sünkel and Mark Stemmler -- What factors protect adolescent bullies from developing into criminal and violent offenders?/Maria M. Ttofi and David P. Farrington -- Cyberbullying: does parental online supervision and youngsters' willingness to report to an adult reduce the risk?/Anna C. Baldry, Anna Sorrentino and David P. Farrington -- Violence risk: the actuarial illusion/David J. Cooke -- The psychopath: continuity or change?: stability of psychopathic traits and predictors of stability/Henriette Bergstrøm, Adelle E. Forth and David P. Farrington -- Policing and detecting deception -- Questioning the interrogational practices of u.s. law-enforcement officers: legal and psychological perspectives/David Walsh, Sean O'Callaghan and Rebecca Milne -- Police interviews of sexually abused children: the state of the art in differentiating truthful and false accounts/Marilena Kyriakidou -- Psychophysiological detection of deception: a review of detection methods, recent research and potential forensic applications/Gershon Ben-Shakhar -- Courts and sentencing -- Wrongful convictions: psychological and criminal justice system contributors/C. Ronald Huff -- The English jury: issues, concerns and future directions/Nicola Padfield -- Extra-legal factors that impact on sentencing decisions/Andreas Kapardis -- Reflections on sentencing in England and Wales/Nicola Padfield. Subjects: Criminal psychology. Criminal behavior. Forensic psychology. Correctional psychology. Notes: Includes bibliographical references and index. Series: Routledge studies in criminal behaviour; 3

*The smoke of London: energy and environment in the early modern city* LCCN: 2016004339 Author/Editor: Cavert, William M., author Main title: The smoke of London: energy and environment in the early modern city/William M. Cavert. Published/Produced: Cambridge: Cambridge University Press, 2016. Description: pages cm. Links: Cover image http://assets.cambridge.org/97811070/73005/cover/9781107073005.jpg ISBN: 9781107073005 (hardback) LC classification: TD884 .C37 2016 Summary: "The Smoke of London uncovers the origins of urban air pollution, two centuries before the industrial revolution. By 1600, London was a fossil-fueled city, its high-sulfur coal a basic necessity for the poor and a source of cheap energy for its growing manufacturing sector. The resulting smoke was found ugly and dangerous throughout the seventeenth and eighteenth centuries, leading to challenges in court, suppression by the crown, doctors' attempts to understand the nature of good air, increasing suburbanization, and changing representations of urban life in poetry and on the London stage. Neither a celebratory account of proto-environmentalism nor a declensionist narrative of degradation, The Smoke of London recovers the seriousness of pre-modern environmental concerns even as it explains their limits and failures. Ultimately, Londoners learned to live with their dirty air, an accommodation that reframes the modern process of urbanization and industrial pollution, both in Britain and beyond"-- Provided by publisher. Contents: Machine generated contents note: Prologue: the smoke of London; Part I. Transformations: 1. The early modernity of London; 2. Fires: London's turn to coal, 1575-1775; 3. Airs: smoke and pollution, 1600-1775; Part II. Contestations: 4. Royal spaces: palaces and brewhouses, 1575-1640; 5. Nuisance and neighbours; 6. Smoke in the scientific revolution; Part III. Fueling Leviathan: 7. The moral economy of fuel: coal, poverty, and necessity; 8. Fueling improvement: development, navigation, and revenue; 9. Regulations: policing markets and suppliers; 10. Protections: the wartime coal trade; Part IV. Accommodations: 11. Evelyn's place: fumifugium and the royal retreat from urban smoke; 12. Representations: coal smoke as urban life; 13. Movements: avoiding the smoky city; Epilogue; Bibliography; Index. Subjects: Smoke--Environmental aspects--England--London--History. Air--Pollution--England--London--History. Air--Pollution--Social aspects--England--London--History. Coal--Environmental aspects--United States. Notes: Includes bibliographical references and index. Series: Cambridge studies in early modern British history

*The women in blue helmets: gender, policing, and the UN's first all-female peacekeeping unit* LCCN: 2016005857 Author/Editor: Pruitt, Lesley J., author. Main title: The women in blue helmets: gender, policing, and the UN's first all-female peacekeeping unit/Lesley J. Pruitt. Published/Produced: Oakland, California: University of California Press, [2016] ©2016 Description: pages cm ISBN: 9780520290600 (cloth) 9780520290617 (pbk.) LC classification: JZ5578 .P78 2016 Summary: "The Women in Blue Helmets tells the story of the first all-female police unit deployed by India to the UN peacekeeping mission in Liberia in January 2007. Lesley J. Pruitt investigates how the unit was originated, developed, and implemented, offering an important historical record of this unique initiative. Examining precedents in policing in the troop-contributing country and recent developments in policing in the host country, the book offers contextually rich examination of all-female units, explores the potential benefits of and challenges to women's participation in peacekeeping, and illuminates broader questions about the relationship between gender, peace, and security."--Provided by publisher. Contents: FFPU in global context -- A brief history of how the FFPU emerged from Indian policing -- Women at work: securing the peace -- Two steps forward and one step back? political economy, women, and violence -- Who's afraid of the girls? -- One size fits some? Subjects: United Nations--Peacekeeping forces. United Nations. Security Council. Resolution 1325. Women and peace. Policewomen. International police. Notes: Includes bibliographical references and index. Additional formats: Online version: Pruitt, Lesley J., author. Women in blue helmets Oakland, California: University of California Press, [2016] 9780520964716 (DLC) 2016007189

*Twilight policing: private security and violence in urban South Africa* LCCN: 2015014686 Author/Editor: Diphoorn, Tessa G., 1984- author. Main title: Twilight policing: private security and violence in urban South Africa/Tessa G. Diphoorn. Published/Produced: Oakland, California: University of California Press, [2016] Description: pages cm ISBN: 9780520287334 (cloth: alk. paper) 0520287339 (cloth: alk. paper) 9780520287341 (pbk.: alk. paper) 0520287347 (pbk.: alk. paper) LC classification: HV8291.S6 D57 2016 Summary: "South Africa boasts the largest private security sector in the entire world, reflecting deep anxieties about violence, security, and governance. Twilight Policing is an ethnographic study of the daily policing practices of armed response officers, a specific type of private security officer, and their interactions with citizens and the state police in Durban, South Africa. This book shows how their policing practices simultaneously undermine and support the state, resulting in actions that are neither public nor private, but something in between, something 'twilight.' Their performances of security are also punitive, disciplinary, and exclusionary, and work to reinforce post-apartheid racial and economic inequalities. Ultimately, Twilight Policing helps to illuminate how citizens survive volatile conditions and to whom they assign the authority to guide them in the process"--Provided by publisher. Contents: Twilight policing: the performance of sovereign power -- "Old school" policing versus "the new South Africa": violence and security in South Africa -- "The promising horse": the armed response sector -- "Wanna-be policemen": being an armed response officer -- "It all comes down to them": daily interactions with the "state" -- "Getting connected with the community": the beneficiaries of armed response -- Performances of twilight policing: public authority, coercion, and moral ordering -- Expanding the twilight. Subjects: Police, Private--Social aspects--South Africa--Durban. Private security services--Social aspects--South Africa--Durban. Notes: Includes bibliographical references and index.

*Virtuous policing: bridging America's gulf between police and populace* LCCN: 2015487601 Author/Editor: Bolgiano, David G., author. Main title: Virtuous policing: bridging America's gulf between police and populace/David G. Bolgiano, L. Morgan Banks, III, James M. Patterson. Published/Produced: Boca Raton [Florida]: CRC Press, [2016] ©2016 Description: xvii, 240 pages: illustrations; 23 cm ISBN: 9781498723503 1498723500 LC classification: HV8138 .B554 2016 Authors: Banks, L. Morgan, III, author. Patterson, James M. (James Michael), 1961- author. Contents: 1. Introduction -- 2. Human operating system 1.0 -- 3. How America treats her warriors and the cults of tribalism and victimology -- 4. Virtuous leadership for law enforcement -- Courage -- Justice -- Self-control -- Competency -- 5. Virtuous policing and Maryland's own NSA -- 6. In defense of self and others in the ghetto: loss of right -- Facts -- discussion -- 30-foot rule explained -- Reasonableness of Tyrone Smith's use of force in defense of others -- 7. Murder in southern California (or cops emulating the TV show Cops) -- Facts -- 8. Officer Ray Bunn and Atlanta's injustice system -- 9. The overutilization of SWAT and the militarization of our police departments -- Fairfax County, Virginia: use of SWAT to kill an optometrist for gambling -- Albuquerque police SWAT arrest a homeless man in a suburban park -- 10. Being poor is not a crime -- 11. Peace officers versus professional law enforcement officers -- 12. When society embraces the bad guys: the sad song of Sergeant Johnnie Riley -- Discussion -- Misunderstanding the tactical dynamics of an encounter -- Action versus reaction -- Fight-or-flight response (emotional intensity) -- Wound ballistics -- How bullets work psychologically -- How bullets work physically -- In defense of self or others -- Mistake belief -- Due process violations -- 13. Redefining the role of state: back to a true liberalism -- 14. Police in our school systems -- Police Athletic League -- Police Explorers -- 15. On notice and the presumption of innocence -- Second Amendment -- Crime and weapons -- 16. How the lack of virtue undermines society itself -- The death of private property rights and America's future -- 17. The power of link analysis -- 18. The ugly and the good in police reformation -- 19. Some solutions -- Developing magnanimity within police officers and departments --

Professionalism in leadership -- Words of caution -- Getting out of the office and vehicles and back into the streets -- Information operations -- Keeping up with the state-of-the-art knowledge: competency in practice -- Fitness for duty -- Force Science Institute courses -- Federal Bureau of Investigation -- Sabbaticals and educational incentives -- Texts and professional reading materials. Subjects: Police--United States. Criminal justice, Administration of--United States. Criminal justice, Administration of. Police. United States. Notes: Includes bibliographical references and index.

*We the people: the modern-day figures who have reshaped and affirmed the founding fathers' vision of America* LCCN: 2016010921 Author/Editor: Williams, Juan, author. Main title: We the people: the modern-day figures who have reshaped and affirmed the founding fathers' vision of America/Juan Williams. Published/Produced: New York: Crown, 2016. Description: pages cm ISBN: 9780307952042 (hardback) LC classification: E169.12 .W535 2016 Summary: "What would the Founding Fathers think about America today? Over 200 years ago the Founders broke away from the tyranny of the British Empire to build a nation based on the principles of freedom, equal rights, and opportunity for all men. But life in the United States today is vastly different from anything the original Founders could have imagined in the late 1700s. The notion of an African-American president of the United States, or a woman such as Condoleezza Rice or Hillary Clinton as Secretary of State, would have been unimaginable to the men who wrote the Declaration of Independence and the Constitution, or who ratified the Constitution or the Bill of Rights. In a fascinating work of history told through a series of in depth profiles, prize-winning journalist, bestselling author, and Fox political analyst Juan Williams takes readers into the life and work of a new generation of American Founders, who honor the original Founders' vision, even as they have quietly led revolutions in American politics, immigration, economics, sexual behavior, and reshaped the landscape of the nation. Among the modern-day pioneers Williams writes about in this compelling new book are the passionate conservative President Reagan; the determined fighters for equal rights, Thurgood Marshall and Martin Luther King, Jr.; the profound imprint of Rev. Billy Graham's evangelism on national politics; the focus on global human rights advocated by First Lady Eleanor Roosevelt; the leaders of the gay community who refused to back down during the Stonewall Riots and brought gay life into America's public square; the re-imagined role of women in contemporary life as shaped by Betty Friedan. Williams reveals how each of these modern-day founders has extended the Founding Fathers original vision and changed fundamental aspects of our country, from immigration, to the role of American labor in the economy, from modern police strategies, to the importance of religion in our political discourse. America in the 21st Century remains rooted in the Great American experiment in democracy that began in 1776. For all the changes our economy and our cultural and demographic make-up, there remains a straight line from the first Founders' original vision, to the principles and ideals of today's courageous modern day pioneers"-- Provided by publisher. "In We the People, renown journalist, Fox political analyst, and bestselling author Juan Williams examines the lives of the men and women in the 20th century who have extended the Founding Fathers' original vision of the country and reshaped what America is"-- Provided by publisher. Contents: The Founding Fathers and Modern America -- THE GREAT AMERICAN MELTING POT: JFK, Ted Kennedy, and the Immigration Reform That Changed America -- THE LIVING CONSTITUTION: Earl Warren, Thurgood Marshall, Martin Luther King Jr., Lyndon Johnson, and the Fight for Civil Rights -- BROKEN WINDOWS, URBAN CRIME, AND HARD DATA: Bill Bratton and Modern Policing -- "NO APOLOGIES, NO REGRETS": General William Westmoreland and the Rebirth of the U.S. Military -- IT'S THE ECONOMY, STUPID: Milton Friedman's New Math of Free Markets, Big Business, and Small Taxes -- LIBERTY AND JUSTICE FOR ALL: Eleanor Roosevelt and the Fight for Global Human Rights -- THE BRIDGE AND TUNNEL CROWD: Robert Moses, William Levitt, and the American City -- "KEEP THE BOYS HAPPY": George Meany, Labor Unions, and the Rise of the Middle Class -- ONE NATION UNDER GOD: Billy Graham and the Power of the Christian Right -- GIRLS TO WOMEN TO YOUR BOSS: Betty Friedan and American Feminism -- THE POWER OF DIPLOMACY: Henry Kissinger, Richard Nixon, and the Opening of China -- ONE-THIRD OF A NATION: Pat Moynihan and the War on Poverty -- EQUAL PROTECTION UNDER THE LAW: Harry Hay, Barry Goldwater, and Gay Rights -- BACK TO THE FUTURE: Ronald Reagan, Ed Meese, and the Remaking of the Judicial System -- THE SOCIAL SAFETY NET: Social Security, Medicare, and Robert Ball -- SILENT SPRING: Rachel Carson and the Environmental Movement -- A NEW BEGINNING -- THE RIGHT TO BEAR ARMS: Charlton Heston and the NRA. Subjects: United States. Constitution. Celebrities--United States--History--20th century. Founding Fathers of the United States. American Dream. History/Social History. United States--Civilization--1970- Notes: Includes bibliographical references and index.

*White-collar crime: the essentials* LCCN: 2016000433 Author/Editor: Payne, Brian K., author. Main title: White-collar crime: the essentials/Brian K. Payne, Old Dominion University, Georgia State University. Edition: Second Edition. Published/Produced: Thousand Oaks: SAGE Publications, Inc., 2016. ©2017 Description: pages cm ISBN: 9781506344775 (pbk.: alk. paper) LC classification: HV6768 .P396 2016 Contents: Introduction and overview of white-collar crime: a systems perspective -- Understanding white-collar crime: definitions, extent, and consequences -- Crimes in sales-related occupation: a systems perspective -- Crimes in the health care system -- Crime in systems of social control: white-collar crime in criminal justice, political, and religious systems -- Crimes in the educational system -- Crime in the economic systems -- Crime in the cyber systems -- Crimes in the housing system -- Crimes by the corporate system -- Environmental crime -- Explaining white-collar crime -- Policing white-collar crime -- Judicial proceedings and white-collar crime -- The corrections subsystem and white-collar crime. Subjects: White collar crimes. Notes: Revised edition of the author's White-collar crime, 2013. Includes bibliographical references and index.

*Who belongs?: race, resources, and tribal citizenship in the native South* LCCN: 2016012095 Author/Editor: Adams, Mikaëla M., author. Main title: Who belongs?: race, resources, and tribal citizenship in the native South/Mikaëla M. Adams. Published/Produced: New York, N.Y.: Oxford University Press, [2016] Description: pages cm ISBN: 9780190619466 LC classification: E93 .A29 2016 Contents: Introduction: citizenship and sovereignty -- Policing belonging, protecting identity: the Pamunkey Indian Tribe of Virginia -- From fluid lists to fixed rolls: the Catawba Indian Nation of South Carolina -- Learning the language of "blood": the Mississippi Band of Choctaw Indians -- Contests of sovereignty: the Eastern Band of Cherokee Indians -- Nation building and self-determination: the Seminole Tribe of Florida and the Miccosukee Tribe of Indians of Florida. Subjects: Indians of North America--Tribal citizenship--Southern States. Indians of North America--Legal status, laws, etc.--Southern States. Indians of North America--Southern States--Politics and government. Indians of North America--Southern States--Government relations. Indians of North America--Kinship--Southern States. Indians of North America--Southern States--Ethnic identity. Federally recognized Indian tribes--Southern States. Notes: Includes bibliographical references and index. Additional formats: Online version: Adams, Mikaëla M., author. Who belongs? New York, N.Y.: Oxford University Press, [2016] 9780190619473 (DLC) 2016014493

*World War I and urban order: the local class politics of national mobilization* LCCN: 2015030903 Author/Editor: Hodges, Adam J. Main title: World War I and urban order: the local class politics of national mobilization/Adam J. Hodges. Published/Produced: New York, NY: Palgrave Macmillan, 2016. Description: pages cm ISBN: 9781137515780 (hardback: alkaline paper) LC classification: D570.85.O81 P674 2016 Variant title: World War 1 and urban order World War One and urban order Scope and content: "This book uses Portland, Oregon to bring to life the transformation of U.S. cities during the first truly national war mobilization effort. World War I had an enormous impact on urban life and the relationship between cities and the federal government that has been almost entirely unexplored until now"-- Provided by publisher. Contents: Portland: middle-class paradise or city of struggle? -- Policing everyday life: federal power, local elites, and citizen spies -- Policing the shipyards: the EFC and the federal struggle for urban industrial order -- Wartime class struggle: the Portland labor movement and the industrial peace regime -- Internment and urban moral order: enemy aliens and "silk stocking girls" -- Postwar clash: the Portland Soviet and the localized struggle over the emergence of communism -- Epilogue. Subjects: World War, 1914-1918--Social aspects--Oregon--Portland. World War, 1914-1918--Political aspects--Oregon--Portland. World War, 1914-1918--Political aspects--United States. Federal-city relations--Oregon--Portland--History--20th century. Federal-city relations--United States--History--20th century. Industrial mobilization--Oregon--Portland--History--20th century. War and society--Oregon--Portland--History--20th century. Social classes--Oregon--Portland--History--20th century. Social control--Oregon--Portland--History--20th century. Portland (Or.)--Social conditions--20th century. Notes: Includes bibliographical references and index.

# RELATED NOVA PUBLICATIONS

## POLICING THE POLICE: KNOWLEDGE MANAGEMENT IN LAW ENFORCEMENT

***Petter Gottschalk (Norwegian School of Management)***
ISBN: 978-1-60741-765-1
Publication Date: 2009

There seems to be a tendency to consider police crime as a result of bad practice, lack of resources or mismanagement, rather than acts of criminals. However, examples illustrate that criminal acts are intentionally carried out by police officers on duty. For example, unauthorized disclosure of confidential information occurred in two out of ten criminal police cases in Norwegian courts in 2007. Police crime does not only occur in countries such as Indonesia, Pakistan, Mexico and Nigeria. It is common in the UK, USA, Australia and Norway as well - although on a smaller scale. Police crime tends to be discovered when investigating police complaints. Police crime is defined as intentional crime committed by police officers on duty. Policing police crime is defined as enforcing law on potential and actual criminal employees in the police organization. Earlier we would say who might watch the watchman, or who is guarding the guardian - now we say who is policing the police. What kind of knowledge management is needed for policing the police? What kind of investigation management is needed for policing the police? What kind of intelligence management is needed for policing the police? What kind of change management is needed to fight police crime? What kind of agency management is needed in policing-the-police organizations? These are questions addressed in this book on Policing the Police - Knowledge Management in Law Enforcement.

## Police Management: Professional Integrity in Policing

***Petter Gottschalk (Norwegian School of Management, Nydalsveien, Norway)***

ISBN: 978-1-60876-903-2
Publication Date: 2010

The prevalence of police deviance is a much-debated statistic and one that is often rife with problems. While some researchers suggest that corruption is endemic to police culture across the globe, others argue that incidents are rare. Despite such statistical problems, incidents of police deviance do surface from time to time all over the world. Some examples in the UK involve suppression of evidence, beating of suspects, tampering with confidential evidence and perjury.

This book addresses these issues and gives the reader insight into the dynamics of police enforcement.

## Community Oriented Policing: Background and Issues

***Jake V. Burke***

ISBN: 978-1-60876-767-0
Publication Date: 2011

Community policing seeks to improve public safety and the quality of life for all persons within the community. Community policing, recognizing that police rarely can solve public safety problems alone, encourages interactive partnerships with relevant stakeholders. The range of potential partners is large and these partnerships can be used to accomplish the two interrelated goals of developing solutions to problems through collaborative problem solving and improving public trust. This book focuses on how police and city leaders can continue to strengthen and add value to local community police efforts. Police and the community work together to identify problems and to respond to community concerns and needs. This includes taking steps to cultivate trusting partnerships in good times, instead of just during a crisis. This book also examines the future of the Community Oriented Policing Services (COPS) program and the authors discuss several important issues that Congress must consider in dealing with this program. This book consists of public documents which have been located, gathered, combined, reformatted, and enhanced with a subject index, selectively edited and bound to provide easy access.

## Exploring Policing, Crime and Society: A Brief but Critical Understanding

***Jason L. Powell (Associate Dean of Faculty, Coventry University, UK)***

ISBN: 978-1-61942-001-4
Publication Date: 2012

This short textbook seeks to provide an conceptual, historical, contemporary and social understanding of the 'police,' one of the key social and legal institutions of the modern state. Police are an integral part of the criminal justice system. On completion of the book, students will have knowledge of the relationship between police, crime and society; the workings, power and discretion of the police; the relationship between policing, social policy and political ideologies. The book is a brief but critical introduction to the main issues facing police officers in the 21st Century.

## Modern Policing: New Paradigms and Perspectives

***Pierce Vertucci***

ISBN: 978-1-62618-017-8
Publication Date: 2013

Effective police leaders become adept at responding to challenge. Like other organizations, police agencies must balance constancy and predictability with adaptation and change. Even as they strive to standardize operations, most police leaders recognize the fluid context in which their agencies operate. They also understand that there are forces to which police organizations must adapt and evolve in order to remain effective in a changing world. It is those forces that drive organizational change and create new models for conducting the business of policing. This book examines the new paradigms and perspectives of modern policing.

## Modern Perspectives on Policing: Selected Papers

***Ryan T. Shwartz***

ISBN: 978-1-63463-969-9
Publication Date: 2015

The boundary between public and private policing is messy and complex. Police executives deal with some aspect of it almost every day. Private investments in security continue to expand and public/private partnerships of myriad types proliferate, even as budgets for public policing stall or decline. This book provides police executives an opportunity to explore the critical issues that arise at this boundary. It also examines policing and wrongful convictions; social media and police leadership; challenges of policing in a democratic society; and costs and value in policing.

## Crime and Violence Prevention: Moving Beyond Hot-Stove Policing and Perpetrator Rehabilitation

***Myra F. Taylor, Umneea Khan, and Julie Ann Pooley (Edith Cowan University, Joondalup, Western Australia, Australia, University of Western Australia, Australia)***

ISBN: 978-1-63483-792-7
Publication Date: 2015

Why do we need to focus on crime and violence prevention in children, adolescents and young adults? Because it is vital to start when offending behaviours first appear. If we fail to stop initial acts of antisocial tendencies and criminality, then these actions become the staging point for a life-long trajectory into adult crime. Breaking the offending cycle during its early stages is one of the most cost effective ways of building a less violent and crime-ridden future society. The reader might well ask: "How is it possible to break the offending cycle and reduce crime on a local, national and international scale?" The well-worn response has oscillated between the introduction of punitive 'harsher penalties' and offender rehabilitation program initiatives. The choice of which of these two approaches holds sway depends on the political agenda of the government in power. Whilst various aspects of each approach have been successful in deterring crime and violence to some extent, they have not been successful enough, as crime and violence perpetration remains a perplexing social issue. What emanates out of the presented research is the emergence of a third global values-driven educative approach to crime and violence prevention, which is slowly beginning to be implemented. This third approach works by challenging and changing the existing pervasive belief that crime and violence are inevitable. The exciting prospect for governments, police, and criminologists is that it is not prohibitively expensive; it complements the existing punitive and rehabilitative approaches, and it is implementable on an offender-by-offender, family-by-family, community-by-community and society-by-society basis. In this regard, examples of current crime and violence prevention initiatives are presented. The book deems which ones are and are not effective in reducing offenses, as well as introduces the steps being considered to introduce a global values-driven educative approach to crime and violence prevention.

## 21st Century Policing: Final Report of the Presidential Task Force and Views on the Future of Community Policing

***Gabrielle M. Schermer***

ISBN: 978-1-63484-102-3
Publication Date: 2016

Trust between law enforcement agencies and the people they protect and serve is essential in a democracy. It is key to the stability of our communi-ties, the integrity of our criminal justice system, and the safe and effective delivery of policing services. In light of events that exposed rifts in the relationships between local police and the communities they protect and serve, President Barack Obama signed an executive order establishing the Task Force on 21st Century Policing. The President charged the task force with identifying best practices and offering recommendations on how policing practices can promote effective crime reduction while building public trust. The recommendations issued by the task force are organized around six main topic areas or "pillars:" Building Trust and Legitimacy, Policy and Oversight, Technology and Social Media, Commu-nity Policing and Crime Reduction, Officer Training and Education, and Officer Safety and Wellness. This book provides an overview of the recommendations of the task force.

## PERSPECTIVES ON POLICING: SELECTED PAPERS ON POLICY, PERFORMANCE AND CRIME PREVENTION

***Holly Wheeler***

ISBN: 978-1-63484-555-7
Publication Date: 2016

Can the police reduce crime? In 1991, when the first Executive Session on Policing concluded, the answer to that question was generally described as being in the eye of the beholder. Based on the scientific and practical knowledge available at the time, some well-respected criminologists and police scholars concluded that the police were not able to reduce crime. Promising evidence, however, suggested that if the police changed their approach to crime control and prevention, then they might be able to reduce crime. This book outlines the changes in the nature of police crime control conversations resulting from an unprecedented growth in rigorous evaluation research on what works in police crime prevention; examines what it means to be a leader within the policing field, and advocates for reframing leadership through the adoption of "learning organizations" to increase the capacity to fight crime; describes "rightful policing," which looks at elements of procedural justice in police encounters with the public as a way to organize police work; advocates for democratic ideals within law enforcement to combat the mindset that law enforcement officers are at war with the people they serve; presents the ideas for what police executives might do to alleviate the problems of race in contemporary policing; examines the term "black-on-black" violence, a simplistic and emotionally charged definition of urban violence that can be problematic when used by political commentators, politicians and police executives; summarizes current understanding of the effects of ongoing trauma on young children, how these effects impair adolescent and young adult functioning, and the possible implications of this for policing; and finally, describes strategies police organizations could employ to more effectively measure their performance.

## COMMUNITY POLICING TO PREVENT VIOLENT EXTREMISM*

### *Dan Silk*

In August 2011, the White House released the important new document "Empowering Local Partners to Prevent Violent Extremism in the United States." This document outlines a broad, outreach-based strategy for reducing the threat of violent extremism.[1] Previous work, including the U.S. National Strategy for Counterterrorism and efforts by the U.S. Homeland Security Advisory Council's Preventing Violent Extremism Working Group and the joint U.S. Department of Justice-U.S. Department of Homeland Security Building Communities of Trust Initiative, supports this document.[2]

The White House document recognizes outreach and community-government relationships as key to successfully protecting the United States from an al Qaeda-inspired threat. The president's introduction to the strategy emphasizes its purpose as outlining "how the federal government will support and help empower American communities and their local partners in their grassroots efforts to prevent violent extremism," which includes "strengthening cooperation with local law enforcement who work with these communities every day."[3] Supported by tactics that closely follow the

* This is an edited, reformatted and augmented version of an FBI Law Enforcement Bulletin publication, dated October 2012, which appeared in *Countering Violent Extremism: Training Efforts and Guidance*, edited by Peter M. Taves, Nova Science Publishers, Inc., 2012.

philosophy of community policing, government-community partnerships represent a vital facet of countering violent extremism.

## TOWARD A NEW PROFESSIONALISM IN POLICING*

### *Christopher Stone and Jeremy Travis*

Across the United States, police organizations are striving for a new professionalism. Their leaders are committing themselves to stricter *accountability* for both their effectiveness and their conduct while they seek to increase their *legitimacy* in the eyes of those they police and to encourage continuous *innovation* in police practices. The traffic in these ideas, policies and practices is now so vigorous across the nation that it suggests a fourth element of this new professionalism: its *national coherence.* These four principles — accountability, legitimacy, innovation and coherence — are not new in themselves, but together they provide an account of developments in policing during the last 20 years that distinguishes the policing of the present era from that of 30, 50 or 100 years ago.

Many U.S. police organizations have realized important aspects of the new professionalism and many more have adopted its underlying values. The ambitions for accountability, legitimacy and innovation unite police organizations in disparate contexts: urban, suburban and rural, municipal, county, state and federal. With approximately 20,000 public police organizations in the United States, national coherence in American policing would be a signal achievement.[1] We do not see this new professionalism fully realized in any single department. We know how difficult it can be to narrow the gap between these ambitions and many deeply ingrained routines and practices. Much policing in the United States remains, in these terms, unprofessional, but professional ambition is itself a powerful force and it is at work almost everywhere.

We hear similar ambitions for accountability, legitimacy, innovation and coherence in other countries, from the state police organizations in Brazil and India to the South African Police Ser v ice, the French Gendarmerie and the Chilean Carabineros. A global police culture with these same four elements

---

* This is an edited, reformatted and augmented version of the National Institute of Justice, NCJ 232359, dated March 2011, which appeared in *Modern Policing: New Paradigms and Perspectives*, edited by Pierce Vertucci, Nova Science Publishers, Inc., 2013.

increasingly defines the ambitions of police leaders in most countries. In this paper, however, we focus on the trend in the United States.

To describe and illustrate the elements of this new professionalism, we draw on our own experiences working in and studying police organizations and on the deliberations of two Executive Sessions on Policing, both convened by the National Institute of Justice and Harvard University's Kennedy School of Government: the first from 1985 to 1992 and the second commencing in 2008 and continuing today.

## Managing the Boundary Between Public and Private Policing*

*Malcolm K. Sparrow*

The boundary between public and private policing is messy and complex. Police executives deal with some aspect of it almost every day. Private investments in security continue to expand and public/private partnerships of myriad types proliferate, even as budgets for public policing stall or decline.

This paper provides police executives an opportunity to explore the critical issues that arise at this boundary. The analysis here starts with a number of assumptions: First, that it is no longer possible for public police to ignore the extent and pervasiveness of private policing arrangements. Second, that being in some general sense "for" or "against" private security is not helpful, as such views are inadequately nuanced or sophisticated given the variety of issues at stake. Third, that the interests of private parties will rarely, if ever, be fully aligned with public interests. Fourth, that it is not sufficient for public police agencies simply to deal with the private security arrangements that exist today; rather, public police have a role to play in influencing future arrangements and in making sure those arrangements serve the public interest.

For the purposes of this discussion, *private policing* is broadly construed and means the *provision of security or policing services other than by public servants in the normal course of their public duties.*

---

* This is an edited, reformatted and augmented version of a paper, NCJ 247182, in the New Perspectives in Policing series, issued by the U.S. Department of Justice, National Institute of Justice, September 2014, which appeared in *Modern Perspectives on Policing: Selected Papers*, edited by Ryan T. Shwartz, Nova Science Publishers, Inc., 2015.

The *clients* for private policing may therefore be public (as with neighborhood patrols) or private (as when corporations contract with private security firms or employ their own security guards).

# POLICING AND WRONGFUL CONVICTIONS*

*Anthony W. Batts, Maddy deLone and Darrel W. Stephens*

Few events subject the criminal justice system to as intense scrutiny from policymakers, elected officials, the media and the general public as the exoneration of a wrongfully convicted defendant. The multimillion-dollar settlement recently announced by New York City in the notorious case of the Central Park Five has once again brought the injustice of wrongful convictions and the corollary injustice of failing to convict the real assailant to the forefront of the national consciousness. (In that case, five black and Latino teenagers were convicted on the basis of false confessions of the brutal — and widely publicized — rape of a young woman jogging in Central Park. All were tried as adults and sentenced to lengthy prison terms, then exonerated years later when the real perpetrator confessed to the crime — a confession corroborated by DNA evidence.) As this and other high-profile wrongful convictions continue to spark controversy, a dispassionate, thoughtful examination of the systemic causes of wrongful convictions and their potential solutions can benefit all components of the criminal justice system and the community at large.

Given their function as gatekeepers to the criminal justice system and as the initial point of contact with offenders, accused offenders, victims and ordinary citizens, police agencies are in the most advantageous position to conduct such an examination. This paper calls for strong leadership from police agencies to lead reviews of wrongful convictions that can be learning experiences for all components of the criminal justice system. The lessons learned from these reviews can lead to the implementation of changes in

* This is an edited, reformatted and augmented version of a paper, NCJ 246328, in the New Perspectives in Policing series, issued by the U.S. Department of Justice, National Institute of Justice, August 2014, which appeared in *Modern Perspectives on Policing: Selected Papers*, edited by Ryan T. Shwartz, Nova Science Publishers, Inc., 2015.

practice across criminal justice agencies that will improve justice without compromising safety.

Section I reviews what has been learned from studying exonerations over the past 20 years, including who the exonerees are, the factors that contribute to wrongful convictions, and the best practices that address these factors. Section II looks at the role cognitive biases play in wrongful convictions. Section III presents several recommendations that research shows will minimize the likelihood of wrongful convictions and that are important for police departments to adopt. These recommendations include best practices that address known contributing factors, including eyewitness identification, false confessions, informant testimony and evidence preservation. This section also suggests an approach for learning from error and viewing mistakes as systemwide weaknesses. Section IV provides suggestions for how police can cooperate and assist with post-conviction investigations and work with other stakeholders to uncover past errors. The conclusion explains why adopting these recommendations will provide both justice and public safety advantages: (1) they will minimize the number of innocent individuals who are wrongly convicted and (2) they will prevent police from overlooking the actual perpetrator early in an investigation because of misleading evidence that points to the wrong person, thereby increasing the number of perpetrators correctly identified in the initial stage.

The recommendations are comprehensive, far-reaching, and necessitate strong leadership from police agencies, both to implement and to provide the guidance required for the entire criminal justice community to adopt a more systemwide approach to learning from wrongful convictions and to improve the system as a whole.

# THE CHALLENGE OF POLICING IN A DEMOCRATIC SOCIETY: A PERSONAL JOURNEY TOWARD UNDERSTANDING*

***Charles H. Ramsey***

> "As a law enforcement officer my fundamental duty is to serve mankind; to safeguard lives and property; to protect the innocent against deception, the weak against oppression or intimidation, the peaceful against violence and disorder; and to protect the Constitutional rights of all people to liberty, equality and justice."

This paragraph is part of the Law Enforcement Code of Ethics (author unknown). I believe it captures the essence of what it means to be a police officer in a democratic society. Unfortunately, the policing profession sometimes loses sight of what I believe is the most challenging element: "to protect the Constitutional rights of all people to liberty, equality and justice."

Police leaders must ensure that their officers fully understand the nature and significance of the commitment this brief phrase suggests. It commits us to a pact with the communities we serve. We make this commitment standing before God, swearing allegiance to the principles, values and ethics of the law enforcement profession.

It took me almost 30 years and a visit to the United States Holocaust Memorial Museum to fully comprehend the role police play in protecting the freedoms that we, as Americans, hold dear. Today, I strive to share important lessons about these obligations with my officers — in part through the use of symbolism and ceremonies and in part by telling certain stories. This paper describes some of the most valuable lessons I believe I learned through reflecting on the exhibits at the Holocaust Museum. It also describes some of the ways in which I have sought to convey those les- sons to other officers.

* This is an edited, reformatted and augmented version of a paper, NCJ 245992, in the New Perspectives in Policing series, issued by the U.S. Department of Justice, National Institute of Justice, June 2014, which appeared in *Modern Perspectives on Policing: Selected Papers*, edited by Ryan T. Shwartz, Nova Science Publishers, Inc., 2015.

# MAKING POLICING MORE AFFORDABLE MANAGING COSTS AND MEASURING VALUE IN POLICING*

*George Gascón and Todd Foglesong*

City governments across the United States today are spending a lot more money on policing than they did 25 years ago. According to the U.S. Department of Justice's Bureau of Justice Statistics, public expenditure on policing in the United States more than quadrupled between 1982 and 2006.[1] As figure 1 shows (page 2), proportionally, spending on corrections and judicial functions (courts, prosecution and public defense) increased over this period more than spending on policing. But in the last 10 years, the rate of increase in spending on policing has exceeded the spending rate for corrections and judicial functions. Between 1996 and 2006, spending on the police increased an average of 8.6 percent each year. Controlling for inflation, expenditures in this period increased at an annual average rate of 3.8 percent.

Even before the onset of the financial crisis, rising expenditures on police departments stirred a debate among city managers, elected officials and police chiefs about how best to pay for policing.[2] But the severity of the financial crisis and the speed with which local governments make budgetary decisions have cut short these conversations. Few of the solutions being fashioned today for the high price of policing address the underlying reasons for the accelerated growth in spending. Nor do they assess what this increased spending means for city governments, residents and the future of the profession.

---

* This is an edited, reformatted and augmented version of a paper, NCJ 231096, in the New Perspectives in Policing series, issued by the U.S. Department of Justice, National Institute of Justice, December 2010, which appeared in *Modern Perspectives on Policing: Selected Papers*, edited by Ryan T. Shwartz, Nova Science Publishers, Inc., 2015.

# POLICING AND SPIRITUALITY: BRIDGING THE GAP TO THE END OF CRIME*

***Dr. Ginger Charles*[1] *and Dr. Jonathan Smith*[2]**

[1]Institute for Spirituality and Policing,
Modesto Junior College in Modesto, California, US
[2]Devon and Cornwall Police, UK

To be confronted with tragic, critical incidents on a daily basis. To face human destructiveness and suffering, to defend society, standing between chaos and order in defense of peace; All require a unique type of individual. It is what we, as a society, demand from our law enforcement officers.

Currently in the United States, we are seeing our police officers questioned for using excessive levels of force. There are increasing numbers of violence erupting within our communities from its members who feel our law enforcement officers are "out of control." In a study of 350 United Kingdom police constables, the cost of PTSD, burnout, and stress was in excess of £99 million or $152 million. Forty percent were deemed to be of medium or high risk of PTSD and 13% of respondents had been signed off work with PTSD one or more times usually for 4+ months costing £11,538 per officer per instance.

In this chapter, we explore the budding importance of spirituality as a coping mechanism in police work, a path through the suffering and disorder. If our police officers are feeling isolated, under valued, and sick then how can they protect and serve our communities? Crime and disorder become pronounced in environments where law enforcement becomes dysfunctional. In our research on spirituality and policing in the United States and the United Kingdom common themes illustrate the importance of this coping mechanism, whereby officers feel "connected" to their profession, their work, and their communities. Can we extend this research toward the communities served to connect our police officers with its members to lessen crime and disorder?

* This chapter was originally published in *Spirituality: Global Practices, Societal Attitudes and Effects on Health*, edited by Edith C. Roberts, Nova Science Publishers, Inc., 2015.

# I Believe in the Hot Stove Principle of Crime Prevention Policing … Educating Kids If You Do the Crime You Will Get Burnt: Australian Police Intelligence Officers' Perspectives on Juvenile Crime*


## *Myra F. Taylor, PhD, MPhil, MEd, MSocSc, BGS, Cert Ed, JP*

Edith Cowan University, Joondalup, Western Australia, Australia



While the literature is replete with studies that have analysed police arrest/charge data as well as a smaller number of studies that have reported on offenders' attitudes towards police, there is surprisingly little research on police perspectives on juvenile crime prevention. To provide some insight into the problems that police experience in dealing with juvenile offenders this chapter utilizes Grounded Theory's inductive approach to the analysis of 10 Australian police intelligence officers' in-depth interviews. The officers who worked in specialty graffiti/rail crime investigation units identified 12 problems with the current approach to juvenile crime prevention (i.e., growing numbers of middle-class juvenile offenders; fractured families; social marginalization; a judicial lack of local knowledge in relation to offenders' home circumstances; juvenile offenders' lack of parental boundaries; affluent and non-affluent parents' differing approaches towards dealing with their offspring's offending; courts imposition of ineffectual slap-on-the-wrist penalties; a resultant revolving door pattern of juvenile crime; juveniles' lack of financial capacity to pay large fines rendering fining an ineffectual punishment; the impracticalities associated with banning juveniles from using public transport; policing difficulties associated with curfews; and the reality that detention centers tend to foster rather than diminish juvenile crime). Three ways of preventing novice offenders from progressing along the pathway to becoming prolific offenders were proposed by police (i.e., increasing the immediacy of police investigations; reducing the time interval between offenders being charged for a crime and their appearance in court; and increasing the opportunities for police to work with the families of novice



* This chapter was originally published in *Crime and Violence Prevention: Moving Beyond Hot-Stove Policing and Perpetrator Rehabilitation,* edited by Myra F. Taylor, Umneea Khan and Julie Ann Pooley, Nova Science Publishers, Inc., 2015.

offenders), as well as three reverse psychosocial ways of preventing prolific juvenile offenders from continuing along a trajectory towards adult offending (i.e., exposing the identity of prolific juvenile offenders; reducing the kudos associated with certain crimes by reframing the charges; and improving parental involvement in crime prevention through making parents financially liable for the damage committed by their offspring). These suggestions are encapsulated in the chapter's core theme, namely that of utilizing the 'hot stove' principle of crime prevention policing.

# FINAL REPORT OF THE PRESIDENT'S TASK FORCE ON 21ST CENTURY POLICING*

## *President's Task Force on 21st Century Policing*

Trust between law enforcement agencies and the people they protect and serve is essential in a democracy. It is key to the stability of our communities, the integrity of our criminal justice system, and the safe and effective delivery of policing services.

In light of recent events that have exposed rifts in the relationships between local police and the communities they protect and serve, on December 18, 2014, President Barack Obama signed an executive order establishing the Task Force on 21st Century Policing. The President charged the task force with identifying best practices and offering recommendations on how policing practices can promote effective crime reduction while building public trust.

This executive summary provides an overview of the recommendations of the task force, which met seven times in January and February of 2015. These listening sessions, held in Washington, D.C.; Phoenix, Arizona; and Cincinnati, Ohio, brought the 11 members of the task force together with more than 100 individuals from diverse stakeholder groups—law enforcement officers and executives, community members, civic leaders, advocates,

---

* This is an edited, reformatted and augmented version of a report issued by the Office of Community Oriented Policing Services, U.S. Department of Justice, May 2015, which appeared in *21st Century Policing: Final Report of the Presidential Task Force and Views on the Future of Community Policing*, edited by Gabrielle M. Schermer, Nova Science Publishers, Inc., 2015.

researchers, academics, and others—in addition to many others who submitted written testimony to study the problems from all perspectives.

The task force recommendations, each with action items, are organized around six main topic areas or "pillars:" Building Trust and Legitimacy, Policy and Oversight, Technology and Social Media, Community Policing and Crime Reduction, Officer Training and Education, and Officer Safety and Wellness.

The task force also offered two overarching recommendations: the President should support the creation of a National Crime and Justice Task Force to examine all areas of criminal justice and propropose reforms; as a corollary to this effort, the task force also recommends that the President support programs that take a comprehensive and inclusive look at community-based initiatives addressing core issues such as poverty, education, and health and safety.

## FUTURE OF COMMUNITY ORIENTED POLICING: SUBMITTED ORAL & WRITTEN TESTIMONY*

### *President's Task Force on 21st Century Policing*

This document contains all Primary Sources for oral and invited written testimony submitted to the Task Force for the listening session on Future of Community Oriented Policing. Five documents are compiled alphabetically by last name when available or by the name of the organization when not provided. A complete list of submissions for A-Z is provided as an easy reference when looking for specific names or organizations.

* This is an edited, reformatted and augmented version of testimony received February 24, 2015 for the seventh and final listening session conducted by the President's Task Force on 21st Century Policing. (Complete details on all seven listening sessions, including submitted documents can be found at the following link: http://www.cops.usdoj.gov/Default.asp?Item=2811), which appeared in *21st Century Policing: Final Report of the Presidential Task Force and Views on the Future of Community Policing*, edited by Gabrielle M. Schermer, Nova Science Publishers, Inc., 2015.

# Community Oriented Policing Services (COPS): In Brief*

*Nathan James*

The Community Oriented Policing Services (COPS) program was created by Title I of the Violent Crime Control and Law Enforcement Act of 1994 (P.L. 103-322). The mission of the COPS program is to advance community policing in all jurisdictions across the United States. The Violence Against Women and Department of Justice Reauthorization Act of 2005 (P.L. 109-162) reauthorized the COPS program for FY2006-FY2009 and changed it from a multi-grant program to a single-grant program. Even though the COPS program is not currently authorized, Congress has continued to appropriate funding for it.

Between FY1995 and FY1999, the annual appropriation for the COPS program averaged nearly $1.4 billion. The relatively high levels of funding during this time period were largely the result of Congress's and the Clinton Administration's efforts to place 100,000 new law enforcement officers on the street. After the initial push to fund 100,000 new law enforcement officers through COPS grants, Congress moved away from providing funding for hiring new law enforcement officers and changed COPS into a conduit for providing federal assistance to support local law enforcement agencies. Decreasing appropriations for hiring programs resulted in decreased funding for the COPS program overall. Appropriations for hiring programs were almost nonexistent from FY2005 to FY2008, but for FY2009 Congress provided $1 billion for hiring programs under the American Recovery and Reinvestment Act of 2009 (P.L. 111-5). Appropriations for hiring programs for FY2009-FY2012 were the result of Congress's efforts to help local law enforcement agencies facing budget cuts as a result of the recession either hire new law enforcement officers or retain officers they might have to lay off. Congress has continued to provide appropriations for hiring programs even though the effects of the recession have waned over the past few fiscal years.

* This is an edited, reformatted and augmented version of a Congressional Research Service publication RL33308, prepared for Members and Committees of Congress, dated January 13, 2015, which appeared in *Law Enforcement Accountability and Public Trust: Federal Regulatory Limits and Financial Tethers*, edited by Shawn W. Nelson, Nova Science Publishers, Inc., 2016.

Authorized funding for the COPS program expired in FY2009. There are several issues policy makers might consider if they take up legislation to reauthorize or fund the COPS program. One potential policy question might be whether the federal government should continue to provide grants to state and local law enforcement agencies to hire additional officers at a time of historically low crime rates. Policy makers might also consider whether Congress should appropriate funding for the COPS program so that law enforcement agencies could take advantage of the current single grant program authorization, or if Congress should continue to appropriate funding for individual programs under the COPS account.

## COMMUNITY ORIENTED POLICING SERVICES (COPS): CURRENT LEGISLATIVE ISSUES*

***Nathan James***

The Community Oriented Policing Services (COPS) program was created by Title I of the Violent Crime Control and Law Enforcement Act of 1994 (P.L. 103-322). The mission of the COPS program is to advance community policing in all jurisdictions across the United States. The Violence Against Women and Department of Justice Reauthorization Act of 2005 (P.L. 109-162) reauthorized the COPS program through FY2009 and changed the COPS program from a multi-grant program to a single-grant program.

The COPS program awards grants to state, local, and tribal law enforcement agencies throughout the United States so they can hire and train law enforcement officers to participate in community policing, purchase and deploy new crime-fighting technologies, and develop and test new and innovative policing strategies. Authorized appropriations for the COPS program expired in FY2009. As such, Congress could consider legislation to reauthorize the COPS program. Debate about reauthorization of the program could be contentious because the COPS program is one of the primary means for providing federal assistance to state and local law enforcement, but at the

* This is an edited, reformatted and augmented version of a Congressional Research Service publication R40709, prepared for Members and Committees of Congress, dated January 13, 2014, which appeared in *Law Enforcement Accountability and Public Trust: Federal Regulatory Limits and Financial Tethers*, edited by Shawn W. Nelson, Nova Science Publishers, Inc., 2016.

same time, Congress is considering ways to reduce discretionary spending in order to shrink the federal budget deficit. This report provides an overview of issues Congress may consider if it chooses to take up legislation to reauthorize the COPS program.

If Congress considers the future of the COPS program, there are several issues it might discuss, including the following:

- Given current trends in violent crime and research findings on the ability of additional law enforcement officers and COPS grants to reduce crime, should Congress consider changing the focus of the COPS program away from providing grants to hire additional officers and toward providing grants to support law enforcement's operations?
- Did the COPS Office meet its goal of placing 100,000 new officers on the street? What does this mean for oversight of the program?
- Are hiring grants a cost-effective way of combating crime?
- Is there programmatic overlap between the COPS Office of Justice Programs (OJP) grant programs?
- Should funding for the COPS program be appropriated as currently authorized in statute?

# CRIME AND POLICING REVISITED*

## *Anthony A. Braga*

Can the police reduce crime? In 1991, when the first Executive Session on Policing concluded, the answer to that question was generally described as being in the eye of the beholder (Sherman, 1992). Based on the scientific and practical knowledge available at the time, some well-respected criminologists and police scholars concluded that the police were not able to reduce crime (Gottfredson and Hirschi, 1990; Bayley, 1994). Promising evidence, however, suggested that if the police changed their approach to crime control and prevention, then they might be able to reduce crime (Goldstein, 1990; Wilson

* This is an edited, reformatted and augmented version of a paper, NCJ 248888, in the New Perspectives in Policing series, issued by the U.S. Department of Justice, National Institute of Justice, September 2015, which appeared in *Perspectives on Policing: Selected Papers on Policy, Performance and Crime Prevention*, edited by Holly Wheeler, Nova Science Publishers, Inc., 2016.

and Kelling, 1982; Sherman, Gartin and Buerger, 1989). In a key Executive Session paper that examined crime and policing, Moore, Trojanowicz and Kelling (1988) highlighted the prospect of improved crime prevention as an explicit goal of community policing by developing problem-solving initiatives to address crime-producing situations and dynamics, stimulating informal social control among residents in high-crime neighborhoods, and apprehending repeat offenders through improved information sharing with the community. Because admittedly little rigorous evidence existed to back their claims.

Moore, Trojanowicz and Kelling's argument was largely regarded as theoretical at the time. As such, the view that tended to dominate most academic and policy discussions at the time was that the police could not reduce crime.

Much has changed since then. A growing body of experiential knowledge and scientific evidence now exists that largely supports many of the key ideas informing innovative crime prevention strategies being discussed in policing circles at the close of the first Executive Session (Skogan and Frydl, 2004; Weisburd and Eck, 2004; Braga, 2008). A review of the available evidence would lead most observers to conclude that the police can reduce crime if they take a focused approach to addressing recurring crime problems, engage the community and a diversity of partners, and implement tactics and strategies appropriately tailored to the conditions that give rise to crime problems. Indeed, when the second Executive Session commenced in 2008, crime control discussions among the participants did not center on the issue of whether the police could reduce crime or not. Rather, conversations focused on how the policing profession could continue effective crime prevention practices by strengthening their commitments to community problem solving and by remaining flexible and adaptable when addressing evolving crime problems.

The stark differences in the nature of the police crime control conversations between the first and second Executive Sessions were the result of an unprecedented period of police innovation and concomitant growth in rigorous evaluation research on what works in police crime prevention. This essay begins by providing a brief historical overview of what was known about the police and crime prevention at the time of the first Executive Session and what were proposed then as promising new ways for the police to reduce crime. Between the 1990s and 2000s, researchers explored the efficacy of these new ideas for crime reduction. Challenges to the notion that innovative policing strategies generate crime reduction gains are then reviewed. The essay concludes by offering two central ideas on continuing effective police crime prevention policies and practices suggested by participants of the second Executive Session and supported by existing research evidence.

# RIGHTFUL POLICING*

## *Tracey L. Meares and Peter Neyroud*

During the summer of 2009, the nation and the world trained their attention on Cambridge, Massachusetts, a small northeastern city of about 100,000 people abutting Boston and home to Harvard University. That summer, a Cambridge police officer arrested renowned Harvard University African American Studies scholar Henry Louis Gates, Jr., who was attempting to enter his home following a long trip abroad. The media were flooded with stories and accounts of "racial profiling," the nature of the problem and the necessity for a national response. Even President Obama famously commented on the incident.[1]

To understand the controversy following Professor Gates's arrest, it is useful to have a factual context: Sergeant James Crowley, the officer who arrested Professor Gates, radioed that he would go to the Gates residence after receiving a dispatch at 12:46 p.m. on July 16, 2009, that a possible breaking and entering was in progress. Crowley arrived to find Gates in his home, and from there the stories diverge. Crowley's version of the events is that Gates was yelling and behaving in a "tumultuous" manner as Crowley attempted to ascertain enough facts to ensure that a crime was not occurring. Gates's view, on the other hand, is that Crowley disrespected him by failing to respond when Gates asked Crowley for his name and badge number. Gates was also upset that Crowley suspected him — a slight, elderly man with a cane — to be a burglar. It is important to emphasize that Sergeant Crowley arrived at Gates's home in response to a 911 call as opposed to an exercise of his own discretion. This point is critical because the typical conception of racial profiling focuses on its legality, and the legality of police action is primarily framed around placing constraints on when police decide to engage people as opposed to how police engage people. Even though his experience fit somewhat uneasily into

* This is an edited, reformatted and augmented version of a paper, NCJ 248411, in the New Perspectives in Policing series, issued by the U.S. Department of Justice, National Institute of Justice, February 2015, which appeared in *Perspectives on Policing: Selected Papers on Policy, Performance and Crime Prevention*, edited by Holly Wheeler, Nova Science Publishers, Inc., 2016.

the typical legal framework of racial profiling, Professor Gates has described his experience in exactly those terms.

How, then, are we to understand the disjuncture between Sergeant Crowley's insistence — as well as the conclusion of many — that he conducted himself lawfully and Professor Gates's insistence that he was unfairly treated and, therefore, racially profiled?

To find an answer, it is necessary to see how two dominant ways of evaluating police leave little room for considering how ordinary people tend to assess their treatment by state authorities. Experts, whether they are police officials or scholars of policing, tend to assess police action eit her w ith respect to its law fulness or w it h respect to its effectiveness at reducing crime and increasing public safety. Police fidelit y to law, especially constitutional law, has long been used as a criterion to distinguish good from bad policing. In addition to the Fourth, Fifth, and Sixth Amendments, other bodies of law — such as police agency administrative regulations, civil lawsuits, or the very law that authorizes police to act in the first place, substantive criminal law — provide standards by which legal authorities measure and assess whether or not policing is carried out properly.[2]

Effectiveness at crime fighting has become the other primary police evaluation metric. Promoted initially by scholars, this yardstick is newer than lawfulness, because for decades many, including police, believed that law enforcement had little impact on crime rates.[3] David Bayley, in his 1994 book, *Police for the Future,* summed up this view nicely:

> The police do not prevent crime. That is one of the best kept secrets of modern life. Experts know it. The police know it, but the public does not know it. Yet, the police pretend that they are society's best defense against crime and continually argue that if they are given more resources, especially personnel, they will be able to protect communities against crime. This is myth.[4]

This is no longer true. Police executives are expected — and expect themselves — to reduce crime rates in their jurisdictions. Policing scholars devote themselves to finding causal connections between various police practices and crime statistics, typically by relying on a theoretical model that assumes offenders are rational actors who are persuaded to desist from criminal behavior when the prospect of formal punishment out weighs the benefits of that behavior. In arresting Professor Gates that day, Sergeant Crowley pursued these two aims of policing simultaneously. He was an assiduous crime fighter, and he acted in a way that was legal. Does that mean that Sergeant Crowley's conduct was unambiguously rightful?

No, it does not. It does not because there is a third way, in addition to lawfulness and effectiveness, to evaluate policing — "rightful policing." Rightful policing attempts to account for what people say that they care about when they assess individual officer behavior as well as agency conduct generally. It differs from lawful policing and effective policing in at least two ways. First, rightful policing does not depend on the lawfulness of police conduct. Rather, it depends primarily on the procedural justice or fairness of that conduct. Second, rightful policing does not depend on an assessment of police as ever more effective crime fighters (although it turns out that rightful policing often leads to more compliance with the law and therefore lower crime rates). This third way may well help us move toward police governance that is substantively, as opposed to rhetorically, democratic. Finally, rightful policing is better for cops on the street. Its precepts not only encourage the people whom police deal with on a daily basis to comply with the law and police directives, they also encourage behaviors in encounters that tend to keep police safe.

## Race and Policing: An Agenda for Action*

***David H. Bayley, Michael A. Davis and Ronald L. Davis***

American police confront issues of race, daily, in almost everything they do. They confront race in the geographic distribution of criminality and the fear of crime as well as in assumptions about what criminals look like. They confront race in the suspicion and hostility of many young African American men they encounter on the street. They confront race in complaints from ethnic communities about being either over- or under-policed. They confront race in charges of racial profiling and unequal justice. And they confront race in decisions about hiring, promoting and assigning police officers. In short, race remains an "American dilemma," as Gunnar Myrdal famously observed in 1944 (Myrdal, 1944), especially and inescapably for today's police.

* This is an edited, reformatted and augmented version of a paper, NCJ 248624, in the New Perspectives in Policing series, issued by the U.S. Department of Justice, National Institute of Justice, June 2015, which appeared in *Perspectives on Policing: Selected Papers on Policy, Performance and Crime Prevention*, edited by Holly Wheeler, Nova Science Publishers, Inc., 2016.

The importance of race in policing has been demonstrated in discussions held since 2008 at the Second Executive Session on Policing and Public Safety at Harvard University. At almost every session, race emerged as a troubling preoccupation for police executives. Although many suggestions for dealing with the issue were discussed, the Executive Session did not try to formulate policies to deal with the various issues involving race. Concern about race seemed to become stalled in discussion rather than advancing to action. So, the authors of this article suggested to the Session members that we try to cull an agenda for action from the years of frank, insightful and sometimes passionate conversation. The Session readily agreed. These are the ideas we think are most promising in terms of what police executives might do to alleviate the problems of race in contemporary policing. They reflect what we have learned that might help the most. We alone are responsible for the contents of this agenda.

Readers should also understand that the agenda consists of suggestions, not directions. Although some of these ideas have been tried, few, if any, have been evaluated. Furthermore, many of them are controversial. We include them nonetheless in order to provoke thought, often explicitly acknowledging their shortcomings. We hope that this agenda will move discussions about race from anger and yearning to concrete action by police leaders, and beyond. This is also not a "scholarly" paper that cites and explores all the writing that has been done on the activities suggested. That is beyond our ability. Therefore, before following any of our leads, readers should do their homework. Others, often more experienced than we, have thought about these issues before.

The agenda is organized into two parts — Strategic Voice and Tactical Agency. Strategic Voice argues that problems of race in policing cannot be resolved by the police alone. Other people must help by understanding and ameliorating the social conditions that cause race to be associated with crime and hence become a dilemma for American policing. Rather than accepting these conditions as givens, police leaders with their powerful collective voice should actively call attention to what needs to be changed.

Tactical Agency outlines what the police can do on their own initiative to deal with the operational dilemmas of race — in the communities they serve and in their own organizations.

# Statement of Matthew Barge, Vice President & Deputy Director, Police Assessment Resource Center. Hearing on "Policing Strategies for the 21$^{st}$ Century"*

Chairman Goodlatte, Ranking Member Conyers, and distinguished members of the Committee:

My name is Matthew Barge. I am the Vice President and Deputy Director of the Police Assessment Resource Center (PARC). I appreciate the opportunity to appear before you and provide an independent perspective on the substantial challenges and opportunities that our local police departments face.

In light of recent high-profile incidents involving local law enforcement agencies and related unrest in several communities across the country, attention has appropriately turned to figuring out what police strategies and approaches best promote effective, safe, and constitutional policing. However, these efforts to identify best practices go back decades.

Some have wondered whether police agencies in our local communities are capable of changing or of proactively reforming themselves. My organization, PARC, has a long history of providing independent, evidence-based counsel on effective, respectful, and publicly accountable policing. A nonprofit organization with offices in New York and Los Angeles, it was founded in 2001 by the Vera Institute of Justice, and with the generous support of the Ford Foundation. PARC is not an advocacy organization. Instead, it is committed to serving as an honest broker that helps law enforcement agencies solve problems by incorporating best practices, managing risks, using data-driven management, and providing services with greater efficiency and accountability. We do all of this with an eye toward increasing officer safety, public safety, and public confidence in the police. PARC has assisted upward of 30 agencies, local governments, or community organizations in these efforts in its 14 years in existence.

In our experience, police departments can change and they are changing. Local governments and police agencies themselves regularly call on PARC to conduct comprehensive assessments of where their departments are, where

* This is an edited, reformatted and augmented version of a statement presented May 19, 2015 before the House Judiciary Committee, which appeared in *Police Use of Force and Federal Tactical Teams: Background and Considerations*, edited by Beverly Guzman, Nova Science Publishers, Inc., 2016.

they should be, and what they need to do in order to align with best practices with respect to accountability and effectiveness. In Portland, Oregon, for example, PARC conducted a review of officer-involved shootings and made recommendations for changes in policy, training, and practice. The implementation of those recommendations led to an 88% drop in officer-involved shootings, a 59% decrease in use of force, and a 51% decrease in citizen s complaints all without increases in officer injuries or crime.[1] Likewise, for some 21 years, Los Angeles County engaged PARC s Executive Director to serve as special counsel for monitoring the Los Angeles County Sheriff's Department, the fourth-largest law enforcement agency in the U.S. The effort produced results with respect to officer training, citizen s complaints, medical care in jails, recruitment and hiring, anti-gang strategies, and many other areas.[2]

In some instances, however, more sustained attention at the national level is necessary. One consequence of our democracy is that police authority is highly fragmented. The most recent data indicate that we have more than 12,000 local police departments that employ roughly 477,000 full-time police officers. Nearly half of these departments employ no more than 10 officers.[3] Some departments fail to identify problems in their relationship with the community, deficiencies in officer oversight, or problems in how its officers use force or detain subjects. Many departments either do not have access to enough useful information about [law] suits involving their officers or intentionally ignore information from suits relating to problematic incidents.[4] Patterns or practices of unlawful policing can take hold.

When problems fester in local police departments, the U.S. Department of Justice (DOJ) may exercise the authority granted by this body[5] to conduct an investigation into alleged patterns of misconduct within a police department with respect to excessive force, discriminatory policing, unlawful stops and searches, and other constitutional violations. Where the allegations are substantiated, those investigations can lead to agreements between the Department of Justice and the involved local jurisdiction, with input from community stakeholders, to implement a package of reforms and remedial measures.

Some of the DOJ settlements take the form of federal-court-overseen consent decrees. The consent decree process is akin to emergency open-heart surgery for police departments. It addresses serious, systemic issues that have built up over time. It is a major intervention that, historically, the Department of Justice has used selectively, at critical moments, and where rigorous and sustained intervention is needed. It is intended to last no longer, but end no sooner, than it takes for the identified problems to be effectively remedied while ensuring officer and public safety. In the past three years, DOJ successfully concluded implementation of two major consent decrees addressing the Los Angeles Police Department and District of Columbia Metropolitan Police Department.

Currently, the Department of Justice is enforcing ten federal-court-overseen consent decrees. PARCs Executive Director, Merrick Bobb, serves as the federal court-appointed, independent monitor of one of those decrees, which relates to the Seattle Police Department (SPD). I serve as his deputy, overseeing a nationwide network of law enforcement experts. Mr. Bobb has nearly 25 years of experience with law enforcement issues, starting with the blue-ribbon commission chaired by Warren Christopher to reform the Los Angeles Police Department (LAPD) in the wake of the Rodney King incident in the early 1990s.

Whether reform is self-initiated, occurs to conform with national standards like those of the Commission on Accreditation for Law Enforcement Agencies (CALEA), or occurs pursuant to a federal investigation or DOJ settlement, the bedrock of policing in the $21^{st}$ century must be a strong, responsive relationship between the nations police departments and the communities that they serve.

To that end, a common playbook of specific, real-world practices and reforms is emerging for ensuring the safety of the public and officers, advance efficient law enforcement, protect constitutional rights, and enhance public trust in the police across America s diverse communities. The challenges are substantial, and the work is hard but law enforcement agencies can today make reforms that we know work in order to enhance accountability and trust. The remainder of my testimony will summarize these areas.

# Statement of Sue Rahr, Executive Director, Washington State Criminal Justice Training Commission. Hearing on "Policing Strategies for the 21st Century"*

Public trust in American policing has been shaken across the nation by the images filling the airwaves beginning in Ferguson last summer and continuing with each new disturbing video that emerges every couple of weeks. These tragic incidents have sparked intense focus on the culture and practices of policing and has ignited a necessary national conversation. As we embark on this dialog it is critically important to consider the wide range of factors that impact the environment in which police operate and consider strategies that are most likely to increase public trust and improve public safety. I'd like to highlight two of the major factors.

The first factor is the absence of a national coherence in policing. We have 18,000 local police departments. That means 18,000 different cultures reflecting the policies and practices that are the product of 18,000 local governments serving communities with a diverse range of values and expectations. Agency size ranges from one-officer to more than 34,000. About half of the 18,000 agencies have less than 10 officers. All of those agencies operate in one of 50 states, each with their unique system of justice that dictates how criminal cases are initiated, processed, and adjudicated. Although many states mandate peace officer certification and standards for hiring and training, most states exert limited control over the routine operations of local police departments. Outside of Consent Decrees and the distribution or withholding of Federal funds, the influence the Federal Government has on local policing is also limited. Bottom line – there is no single description of police culture and practice in the United States. The environments and challenges faced by police departments vary widely, and control and oversight is almost exclusively local.

The second factor to consider is that police departments do not operate independently. In most cities, Police Chiefs are hired and fired by a Mayor, or another elected Municipal Executive. Most Sheriffs are elected by the voters they are sworn to serve and protect. When police exert control over citizens,

---

* This is an edited, reformatted and augmented version of a statement presented May 19, 2015 before the House Judiciary Committee, which appeared in *Police Use of Force and Federal Tactical Teams: Background and Considerations*, edited by Beverly Guzman, Nova Science Publishers, Inc., 2016.

they do so at the behest of officials elected by the people. Crime control strategies don't emerge in isolation. Nor do decisions about police accountability. Those decisions are made by independently elected local officials and Prosecutors. Too often the scrutiny of disturbing incidents begins and ends with the police department with little examination into those forces outside the agency that influence priorities and practices. The importance of a broader focus of inquiry was illustrated by the recent examination by the Department of Justice into the government practices in the City of Ferguson. The findings serve as a powerful example of the influence of governing forces outside of the police department itself.

Ideas for improving policing in the 21st Century need to be considered with these two important factors in mind. Most changes in policies and procedures must be adopted by local governments in order to be implemented. For example, a requirement to use body cameras must consider local and state laws related to the gathering, management, and disclosure of data as well as local and state laws protecting individual privacy. These changes will take time and require changes in state laws, with some barriers simply insurmountable.

There are, however, meaningful steps that can be taken at various levels of government, without changing laws. These steps will improve the culture of policing and expand police training in ways that contribute to increased public trust and improve public safety. The recommendations of the President's Task Force on 21st Century Policing contain a range of actions that can be implemented immediately, as well as longer term strategies.

# INDEX

## C

## D

## E



## F



## G

## H



## I

## J



## K



## L



## M

## N



## O



## P

## Q



## R

## S

## T



## U

## V



## W



## Y



## Z